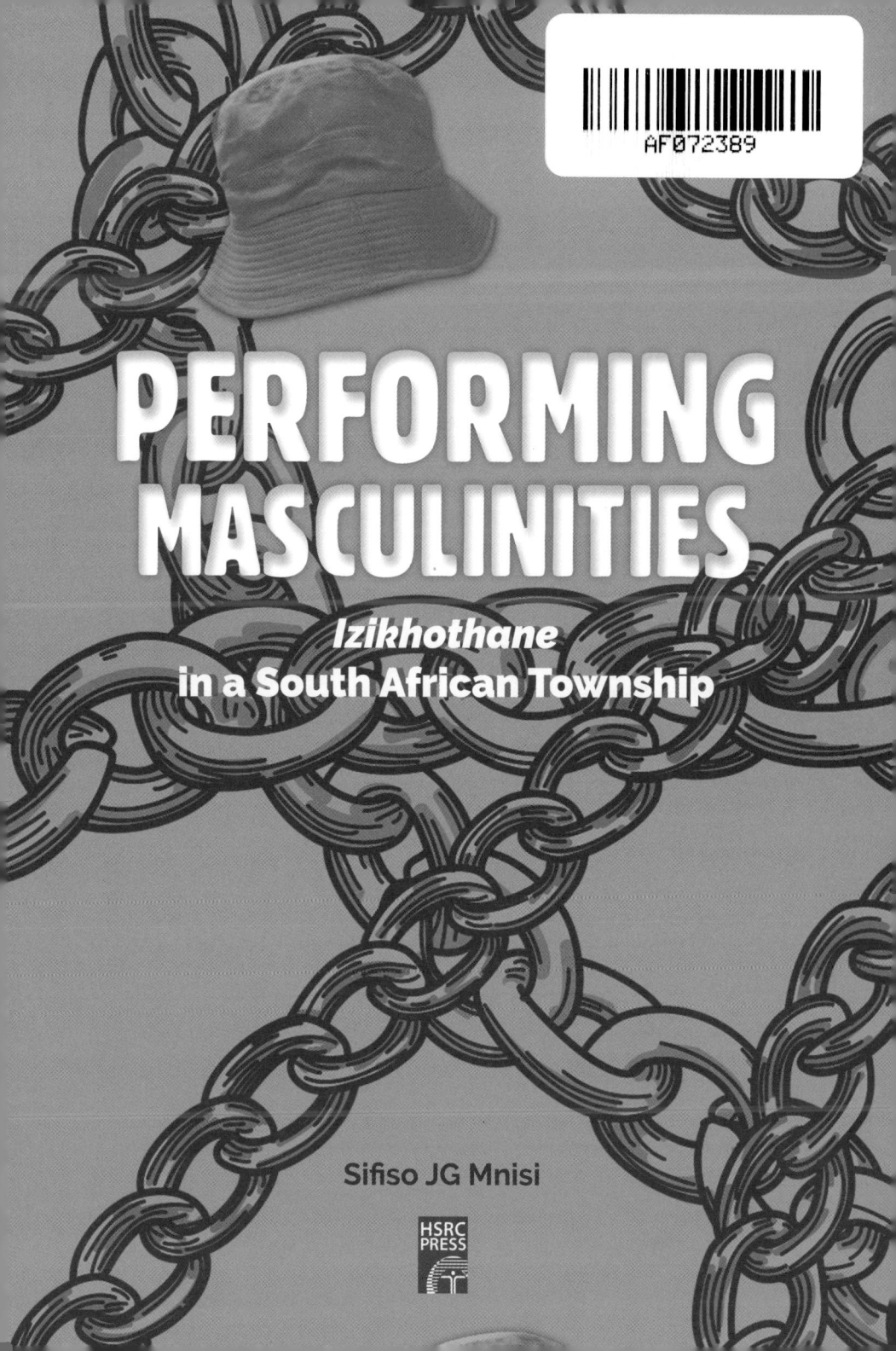

PERFORMING MASCULINITIES

Izikhothane in a South African Township

Sifiso JG Mnisi

HSRC PRESS

Published by HSRC Press
Private Bag X9182, Cape Town, 8000, South Africa
www.hsrcpress.ac.za

First published 2025

ISBN (soft cover) 978-0-7969-2686-9
ISBN (pdf) 978-0-7969-2687-6

© 2025 Human Sciences Research Council

This book has undergone a double-blind independent peer-review process overseen by the HSRC Press Editorial Board.

The views expressed in this publication are those of the author. They do not necessarily reflect the views or policies of the Human Sciences Research Council (the Council) or indicate that the Council endorses the views of the author. In quoting from this publication, readers are advised to attribute the source of the information to the individual author concerned and not to the Council.

The publishers have no responsibility for the continued existence or accuracy of URLs for external or third-party Internet websites referred to in this book and do not guarantee that any content on such websites is, or will remain, accurate or appropriate.

Copy-edited by Liz Sparg
Typeset by Clinton Griffin
Cover design by Zama Nsutsha
Printed by [Name of printer, city, country]

Distributed in Africa by Blue Weaver
Tel: +27 (021) 701 4477; Fax Local: (021) 701 7302
www.blueweaver.co.za

Distributed worldwide (except central and southern Africa)
by Lynne Rienner Publishers, Inc.
Tel: +1 303-444-6684; Fax: +1 303-444-0824; Email: cservice@rienner.com
www.rienner.com

No part of this publication may be reproduced, stored in a retrieval system, or transmitted by any form or by any means, electronic, mechanical, photocopying, recording or otherwise, without prior permission from the copyright owner.
To copy any part of this publication, you may contact DALRO for information and copyright clearance.

Tel: 086 12 DALRO (or 086 12 3256 from within South Africa); +27 (0)11 712-8000
Fax: +27 (0)11 403-9094 Postal Address: P O Box 31627, Braamfontein, 2017, South Africa www.dalro.co.za

Any unauthorised copying could lead to civil liability and/or criminal sanctions.

Suggested citation: Mnisi SJG (2025) *Performing Masculinities: Izikhothane in a South African Township.* Cape Town: HSRC Press

Contents

List of figures   iv
Preface   v
Acknowledgements   viii

1   *Ukukhothana*: A post-apartheid subculture   1
2   Academic perspectives on *ukukhothana*   7
3   Consumption, masculinities and *izikhothane*   24
4   Rehumanisation through consumption   47
5   Booty on fire: Looking at *izikhothane* through Veblen's lens   63
6   Burning to consume? Conspicuous consumption versus aspirational consumption   75
7   On gender performativity: Masculinities and social psychology   91
8   Aspirational masculinities: Consumption, masculinities and being a Good Fella   103
9   Consumption and social change   126
10   Conclusion: Is manhood for sale?   140

Bibliography   145
About the author   158
Index   159

List of figures

Figure 6.1	Proposed framework of BoP aspirational consumption	82
Figure 7.1	Vega and his family	98
Figure 8.1	Rabbi at his matric farewell party	105
Figure 8.2	Vega posing with his glass during the matric farewell ceremony	107
Figure 8.3	Mpho (Sekatana) and Tshepo walking to Festival Mall in Kempton Park	110
Figure 8.4	Bambo at the Festival Mall Ice Rink	111
Figure 8.5	Audience inside the Sam Hlalele Hall at the 2018 Miss Masakhane Beauty Pageant	120
Figure 8.6	The Good Fellas come on stage to perform at the 2018 Miss Masakhane Beauty Pageant	120
Figure 8.7	RLYF Facebook post	121
Figure 9.1	Manqoba at his car wash in Phomolong	137

Preface

This book delves into the complex layers of identity, expression and societal dynamics. It is an invitation to engage with a phenomenon that has captured the attention of scholars, cultural critics and communities alike. This preface serves as a primer, introducing the reader to the rich tapestry of themes and perspectives explored within the following chapters.

Appearing wealthy at the expense of pursuing possible wealth-creation opportunities seems to be a preoccupation among some South African youth. This aspiration, known as *ukukhothana*, leads to behaviour among some people living in poverty, where conspicuous consumption seems to prevail over logical consumption, for example, for sustenance. *Ukukhothana*, a subculture emerging from South African townships, undoubtedly encapsulates a cloud of confusion in post-apartheid South Africa.

The book is inspired and informed by concerns about the consumption patterns of people living on the margins of the economy in post-apartheid South Africa. It explores township male youth identity formation processes mediated through consumer markets. At the book's core is the desire to investigate how consumption may aid young men's pursuit of masculinities and aspirations in our townships through *ukukhothana* subcultures.

In exploring the intersection of the *ukukhothana* subculture and masculinities, I chose an ethnographic approach to observe and learn about the subculture by following The Good Fellas, a group from Thembisa, the second-largest township in Gauteng. Over 11 months, I conducted group and individual interviews with all 15 group members, attended events they were hosting or invited to, and journaled these observations.

Ukukhothana embodies a unique fusion of performance, materialism and contestation of societal norms. At its core, the *ukukhothana* subculture challenges traditional notions of masculinity, offering a lens through which to examine the intricacies of gender, power and self-identity in contemporary society.

The chapters navigate the historical roots of *ukukhothana*, tracing its evolution from its origins in the townships to its present-day manifestations. I unpack the performative elements of *ukukhothana*, exploring the significance of fashion, dance and public displays of wealth as modes of expression and assertions of identity. Through the voices of participants and observers, I gain insight into the motivations driving the practices of the *izikhothane* (those who practice *ukukhothana*) and the meanings imbued therein.

Central to my exploration is the interrogation of masculinities within the subculture. I seek to challenge conventional understandings of masculinity as static and monolithic, instead highlighting its fluidity and multiplicity. By examining the *izikhothane* performances of gender, I illuminate how individuals negotiate and contest societal expectations of what it means to be a man. Importantly, this book does not seek to romanticise or sensationalise the subculture, but to critically analyse its social, cultural and political dimensions. I acknowledge the complexities and contradictions inherent within the subculture, as well as the broader implications for the South African society at large.

The strength of this book is in documenting one of the most important and bizarre subcultures emerging from South African townships after 1994. While conversing with scholarship on masculinities, subcultures, social class and youth studies, I seek to provide a unique synthesis of all these ideas as evidenced in the activities of the *izikhothane*. The book contributes to scholarship that seeks to understand the unique link between masculinities and consumption among township youths, particularly within the context of a subculture. While the literature on men and masculinity is growing, the field in South Africa is arguably at the infant stage. Thus, this book is poised to contribute to these conversations.

In the following chapters, I grapple with what it means to be a man in a South African township in relation to consumption. Thus, the subsequent chapters explore the idea of consumption as a unique avenue to seek, attain and perform a plethora of masculinities through historical references, political transitions and socioeconomic realities in both lived and imagined experiences.

As I embark on this exploration, I invite readers to approach the subject matter with an open mind and a willingness to engage with the complexities of identity, power, consumption and representation. I hope this book will spark dialogue, challenge assumptions, and contribute to a deeper understanding of *ukukhothana* and its implications for constructing masculinities in contemporary South African townships.

Acknowledgements

I want to express my gratitude to The Good Fellas because, without them, the insights presented in this book would not have been possible. Thank you – *zimbidla zam!*

1 Ukukhothana: *A post-apartheid subculture*

The early 2000s saw the emergence of a bizarre subculture in some South African Townships, known as *ukukhothana*, practised by *izikhothane*. Adherents to this 'youth craze' are predominantly black township male youths, typically between the ages of 13 and 22, who engage in destructive conspicuous consumption. The term *izikhothane* may have originated from a loose translation of the Caribbean British 'The Lickers', who trump, beat or outdo others.[1] The subculture of *ukukhothana* further alludes to the Afro-American trend of 'dissing' or displaying disrespectful conduct (Nkosi 2011).

The subculture entails regular social gatherings on weekends in which groups of *izikhothane*, most of whom are still in high school, compete in mock battles. They show up at street events wearing expensive designer labels such as Rossimoda shoes, DMD shirts, Versace, and expensive sportswear. They also bring takeaway food such as KFC and Debonair's Pizza, and the popular South African favourite dessert, Ultra Mel Custard, perceived in the townships as luxury foods. Popular, expensive alcohol brands such as Bisquit Hennessy and Jameson, traditionally associated with affluent people, accompany the food.

In front of a cheering audience and with loud music to heighten the pleasure at these gatherings, *izikhothane* sometimes tear, burn or trample on the expensive clothes; they also throw their favourite food on the ground and at each other in a playful and boastful manner. Further, they occasionally drink the alcohol from their shoes, pour it on the ground, and even use it to wash hands. *Izikhothane* also scatter bank notes on the dusty streets and set them on fire. Interestingly, they use the Ultra Mel custard to write the group's name on the ground, making their mark as *izikhothane*. This behaviour is intended to show off wealth and style and to outdo each other in attracting cheers from the audience, attention from female spectators and respect from rival groups of *izikhothane*. However, it is not anti-consumption behaviour, as this book will detail.

What makes *izikhothane* fascinating is the stark contrast between their public performances of destructive conspicuous consumption and their lived experiences, underscored by economic impoverishment and working-class realities of relative scarcity. *Izikhothane* are predominantly from working-class families, whose parents, if employed, are domestic workers, drivers, gardeners or informal business owners. Some adherents to the subculture are orphans from child-headed households, forced to fend for themselves by selling essentials, washing cars, or working in the informal business sector. Some families depend on meagre social security grants.

The obvious questions that arise in the face of this astounding subculture are: 'Why waste the few resources you have?', 'How do *izikhothane* afford to fund their destructive habits, given their socioeconomic status?', 'What are the benefits of participating in this subculture?', 'Why are the participants mostly males?', and 'Why is the subculture predominantly popular in the townships?'

The topic of consumption in post-apartheid South Africa is a complex one. Any attempt to make sense of it requires a nuanced approach that considers our history, cultures, religions and socioeconomic realities. It demands the ability to imagine the future by looking at the aspirations of our people through the eyes of the youth. In this book, I grapple with questions of identity, notions of masculinity and ideas of 'being' in the township for young men, post-1994, who live in one of the most unequal countries on earth. I explore deeply what it means to be a 'man' to boys growing up in townships. I interrogate ideas of consumption in the context of abject poverty that exists behind a façade of rapid economic transformation within the second-largest economy in Africa.

In doing this, I use the lens of consumption to analyse the performances of masculinities by following the subculture of *ukukhothana*, which in post-apartheid South Africa undoubtedly sparked raging controversy and conversation in various spheres of society. The media reported on the subculture, at first, with curiosity, ambivalence and hysteria. In one instance, Debora Patta, who anchored e.tv's investigative journalism show 3rd *Degree*, on 22 May 2012 described *ukukhothana* as 'bling gone obscenely mad'. The clergy have viewed it as demon possession (Sonti 2020), while civil society has condemned the behaviour as unnecessarily wasteful. Academia also joined the conversation to question and make sense of the subculture by analysing the contextual environments conducive to its development in post-apartheid South African townships. Literature emerged from a broad range of academic fields including anthropology, psychology, fine arts, gender studies, political studies, business studies, communication studies and fashion studies.

Given the relative newness of *ukukhothana*, as far as academic inquiry is concerned, this book draws from rich ethnographic research conducted in the township of Thembisa. This township is in the East Rand of Gauteng Province, affectionately known as *eGoli*, or the 'City of Gold' due to the gold mining industry that blossomed in the late 1800s. In this book, I document the subculture of *ukukhothana* by following The Good Fellas in Thembisa.

Thembisa: Nexus of izikhothane

Thembisa is in the north of Kempton Park and falls under the Ekurhuleni Municipality in Gauteng. It is the second-largest township in the province after Soweto. It was founded in 1957 under the National Party government's Group Areas Act to accommodate black people displaced through forced removals from areas that became white suburbs and industrial sites. These areas, created as part of apartheid's vision of separate development, included Edenvale, Kempton Park, Midrand and Germiston (South African History Online 2019).

The name Thembisa, which means promise, comes from isiXhosa, one of the 12 official languages in South Africa. Presumably, the creation of this township was meant to represent hope for those who had become displaced and homeless. Initially 'Thembisa', the spelling changed twice with demographical changes. With an influx of migrants who spoke various languages from the northern region, the name became 'Tembisa' (South African History Online 2019). However, in February 2020, the township reverted to its original name, 'Thembisa'.

Similar to other South African townships, Thembisa's history is associated with black suffering under the apartheid regime. Stark levels of economic inequality continue to plague the township long after the dawn of democracy. This context is highly significant to this study, with its focus on post-apartheid South Africa and black middle-class aspirations, an idea that has received little academic attention in Thembisa.

South African townships are generally divided into four sections. The township suburb is where most of the middle class reside in newly built houses, most of which are financed through home loans or mortgages. The oldest section of the township comprises four-roomed apartheid government-built houses that are the iconic image of the township. Multiple generations have come from this section, so most houses have been renovated and extended. The third section comprises post-apartheid government-built houses as part of the Reconstruction Development Programme (RDP), known as RDP houses; this section usually emerges as an informal settlement but is later developed into RDP houses. The last section is the informal settlement characterised by makeshift shacks with pit toilets and communal taps and lacks essential local government services such as waste management.

This book focuses on three sections of Thembisa: Birch Acres, the township suburb with newly built houses financed through a bank loan – commonly called '*ema new house*' ('new houses') in township slang; Phomolong, comprised of old houses; and Vusimuzi, the informal settlement.

The Good Fellas live in two adjacent township areas, Phomolong and Vusimuzi. Upon entering Thembisa from Kempton Park using the Chloorkop Road, one notices that Phomolong is located on the left-hand side, towards the west of Thembisa, while the more affluent Birch Acres is on the right-hand side. Phomolong has numerous government schools, a library, a clinic, and a taxi rank. In the past, there was a customer care centre known as the Phomolong Pay Point and an old people's home, but both were shut down for unknown reasons. Phomolong boasts informal businesses such as street vendors, street food, and tuck shops (run from cargo containers and garages). Also known as spaza shops, most tuck shops are owned by foreign nationals renting space from local residents who depend greatly on these mini-convenience stores that make small daily household items like bread and utilities such as airtime available. Often referred to as 'my friend' (because they tend to address customers in this way), foreign national tuck shop owners tend to bear the brunt of looting and other atrocities when the occasional xenophobic violence flares up.

The tuck shops are also widely used to access essential services such as withdrawing money, as 'cash backs'. This transaction is similar to withdrawing cash at a till point in a retail store; one swipes the desired amount of cash on the speed point as though making a purchase but receives cash. The popularity of 'cash backs' stems from a scarcity of automatic teller machines (ATMs) due to the notorious ATM bombings, which have plagued most townships in South Africa.

Although most of The Good Fellas crew live in Phomolong, my journey with them began in Vusimuzi, where the remaining members stay or have family ties. One of the group members, Mpho (commonly known as Sekatana), who facilitated my acquaintance with The Good Fellas, lives in Vusimuzi. The informal settlement of Vusimuzi is awkwardly located next to middle-class Birch Acres. If one considers inequality in terms of social class in post-apartheid South Africa, then Vusimuzi is the epitome of inequality, where most people live below the breadline. It is wedged between a cemetery and overhead power lines, and often experiences flowing sewage streams. Like other informal settlements, it neither has access to the electricity supplied by the power lines nor the sewage system that often plagues it with an unpleasant stench. Vusimuzi dwellers use pit toilets or the red and blue portable non-flush mobile toilets provided by the municipality.

Moav and Neeman, in their 2008 paper titled 'Conspicuous consumption, human capital, and poverty' argue that 'poor families around the world spend a large fraction of their income on consumption of goods that appear to be useless in alleviating poverty' (2008:1). They conclude that individuals living in abject poverty also care about status. Against the backdrop of wealth disparity in Thembisa, specifically the three focus areas – Birch Acres, Phomolong and Vusimuzi – the activities of *izikhothane* give currency to Moav and Neeman's observations. Although the wealthier Birch Acres residents engage in conspicuous consumption, they are seemingly outdone by their less well-off neighbours. No known crews of *izikhothane* in Birch Acres could rival the conspicuous consumption of The Good Fellas, hence their popularity and status in the area.

The Good Fellas

The Good Fellas is an all-male, 14-member crew of *izikhothane* from Thembisa. Their name originated with an older crew of the *amapantsula* subculture that was popular in the area in the early 2000s. The *pantsula* subculture first emerged in Johannesburg's townships, mainly in Alexandra and Sophiatown, during the 1950s as a response to forced removals. Initially understood to be a subversion of political authority and oppression, it has changed over the years. In the early days, practitioners of the subculture were 30 years of age and above; this changed to 30 and below. However, *amapantsulas'* love of fashion has remained unchanged. *Pantsula* was always known for dance and dress, and in the 1990s, it came to be closely associated with *kwaito* music; the wearing of Converse All-Star sneakers, khaki pants and soft cotton bucket hats known as *ispoti*; as well as with the *tsotsitaal* (slang language associated with criminal gangs, or *tsotsis*, which is a mixture of Afrikaans, vernacular, and occasionally English).[2] At one point, the members of *Pantsula* were perceived as gangsters and accused of engaging in criminal activities, a narrative they denied (Kuta 2019).

The preoccupation of *amapantsulas* with dance and fashion is one of the common aspects between this subculture and *izikhothane*. In another shared similarity, *izikhothane* have also been accused of criminality. Although *izikhothane* are unique in their activities, they exist in a long continuum of township subcultures.

Notes
1 Martin Z (2011) UNCUT Izikhothane, June/July 2011: 29–30
2 The evolution of the pantsula subculture. *Unlabelled X Lure.*
   Accessed 28 September 2019, https://www.unlabelledmagazine.com/post/2019/03/01/the-evolution-of-the-pantsula-subculture-unlabelled-x-lure

2 *Academic perspectives on* ukukhothana

The novelty of *ukukhothana* implies that academic research on the subculture is scant. As a result, previous research has heavily relied on media reports, which focused mainly on its notorious aspects, particularly in 2011 and 2012, when the subculture was reported to be at its 'height'. The earliest study of *ukukhothana* was Penelope Mkhwanazi's master's thesis in Business Administration, titled 'Conspicuous Consumption and Black Youth in Emerging Markets', completed at the University of Pretoria's Gordon Institute of Business Science (GIBS) in November 2011.

Mkhwanazi, who refers to *ukukhothana* as *pexing*, notes that what the subculture is called varies from township to township, probably due to the different languages that dominate. Following Dinu and Tanase (2010), Mkhwanazi (2011: 3) uses postmodernism to study *pexas* from Soshanguve township, north of Pretoria, and to explore conspicuous consumption among black youths in emerging markets. Mkhwanazi (2011: 18) defines postmodernism as a 'framework that facilitates the dissemination and understanding of complex changes taking place in society'. She identifies several key characteristics of *pexing*.

Firstly, Mkhwanazi argues that even though *pexing* is similar to conspicuous consumption, it has many aspects that distinguish it from Veblen's (1899) conception of the leisure class. In particular, the aspect of destruction amid poverty makes it difficult to speak of *pexing* exclusively as conspicuous consumption. Mkhwanazi (2011: 132) calls it 'destructive conspicuous consumption' and argues that *pexing* displays practices that could, to a certain extent, be considered anti-consumerism.

The first anti-consumerism practice is avoiding the consumption of certain products, such as cheap clothes, to reinforce a positive identity in terms of social status. The second practice is purchasing a product – only to destroy it in front of an audience – to suggest wealth.

However, Mkhwanazi (2011) notes that these behaviours are different from typical anti-consumerism activities, which are characterised by an outright ideology of rejection. *Pexing* aims to emphasise the cost of the products, and one's ability not only to afford to purchase them but also to destroy them.

Secondly, Mkhwanazi argues that *pexing* is influenced by several life events: a low-income environment; the life stage in which the participants find themselves; and the social structure to which they are exposed, that is, the influence that adults have on them regarding consumption. She argues that *pexing* creates a hyper-reality – a momentary fantasy world characterised by objectification – which includes the use of people (for example, girls are often present as cheering bystanders who are impressed and then courted), as well as the taking up of multiple identities, including one of poverty masked by wealth.

Finally, Mkhwanazi finds that there are negative aspects to *pexing*, including participating in crime; physical harm such as suicide; poor academic performance; bullying, insulting and provoking other youths; as well as parents getting heavily indebted from financing their children's participation in the subculture.

However, there is more to be said about the societal structure within which *izikhothane* exist. There is a tendency in post-apartheid South Africa's public discourses and media to 'conflate the capacity to consume with a rhetoric of national prosperity that elides the lacunae between rich and poor' (Jones 2013: 209–10). Jones expands the idea of conspicuous destruction in the activities of *izikhothane* in her 2013 article published in *Safundi: The Journal of South African and American Studies*, titled 'Conspicuous destruction, aspiration and motion in the South African township'. She explores the tension between aspiration and wastefulness as it unfolds in the activities of *izikhothane* – which she spells *i'khothane,* a derivation from the isiZulu spelling to isiXhosa, and that has no significance to the meaning of the subculture itself.

Jones' (2013) article seeks to examine how forms of destruction surface in two South African novels about township life: one set in Umlazi, titled *Young Blood* (2010) by Sifiso Mzobe, and the other set in Soweto, titled

African Cookboy (2010), by David Dinwoodie-Irving. The two novels focus on the accrual of money generated illegally and the resultant social status that follows male protagonists' conspicuous consumption and drag racing. Jones examines the tension between young township people's lives and aspirations. In the case of *izikhothane*, this manifests in the contrast between destructive consumption and the realities that confront them post their fleeting fantasy world.

Jones (2013: 210) notes that there is more to the subculture of *ukukhothana* than destructive behaviour and 'to dismiss *i'khothane* as simply stupid or disgusting is to fail to ask how spatial exclusion continues to operate in South African cities and how such practices might contest the marginalisation of the poor'. She further explores the use of a car as not only a mode of transportation from one point to another but also as a form of social transport symbolically representing upward social mobility. She alludes to the use of cars in the township to symbolise a certain level of success, thus generating a high social status for those who possess them. Concerning drag racing, she explains that the novels she discusses speak to the gesture that vies for visibility amid struggles against poverty, crime, and unemployment and concludes:

> modes of exhibition such as i'khothane speak to the processes through which severe social and economic pressures are folded into and negotiated through daily life. They expose and confirm a dialectical tension between the enunciating capacities of ikasi [the township] style and the structural inequalities persisting in South Africa's city spaces. (Jones 2013: 223)

In the following section, I explore the role of activities that young people choose in forging their desired identities.

Conspicuous consumption is modelled in the township

Identity formation, which culminates in its expression, is a significant process for young people, and it is always influenced by context. Malosa Langa expresses the significance of this process in his 2012 doctoral thesis titled 'Becoming a Man: Exploring Multiple Voices of

Masculinity Amongst a Group of Young Adolescent Boys in Alexandra Township, South Africa', in which he notes that 'the process of identity formation differs over time and context. Each context gives the youth the structure within which to forge different kinds of identities' (Langa 2012: 16). In line with this perspective, Howell and Vincent (2014: 60) assert that the practice of *ukukhothana* 'is a potent means of articulating youth identity in settings seemingly left behind by the "new" South Africa'.

Howell and Vincent (2014) conducted a study with seven young men who identified as members of a crew of *izikhothane* from the Eastern Cape. They used qualitative in-depth interviews with group members in English with a translator present to assist where necessary. Their analysis of the interviews is informed by drawing on the work of various authors from the fields of consumption, cultural and township studies. Howell and Vincent (2014) argue that the prominence of 'black diamonds' has provided symbolic role models for the youth, most of whom have consistently been excluded from South Africa's economic development. Black diamonds are the professional, powerful and extremely wealthy few who have benefited disproportionately from South Africa's economic redistribution effort. Being an *izikhothane* is one way in which less wealthy black young men deal with what it means to be young and poor in an economically unequal post-apartheid South Africa. Howell and Vincent (2014: 62) observe that the show of wealth is linked to *izikhothane* paying homage to what they perceive to be the meaning of masculinity in a democratic dispensation, which is associated with material success and sexual conquest.

In the interviews, group members remarked that the destruction of their expensive possessions happened primarily to acquire respect and social status. In the process, they also attracted women and enjoyed themselves. Howell and Vincent (2014: 65) note that the members go to great lengths to attain symbols of wealth that make them worthy objects of respect and enable them to emulate public figures such as Kenny Kunene, a wealthy businessman who made headlines for eating sushi off a naked model at his nightclub in Sandton, and hence known as the 'Sushi King'.[1] The authors further note that the destruction of valuables accumulated under difficult situations is a form of mockery of capitalism, whose system of meaning is momentarily transcended. This observation is reminiscent of the notion of anti-consumerism behaviour.

Chipp, Kapelianis and Mkhwanazi (2015) make a related observation in a paper titled '*Ukukhothana*: The Curious Case of Conspicuous Consumption and Destruction in an Emerging Economy'. Chipp et al. (2015) note that the destructive activities of *izikhothane* are not the conventional type of anti-consumerism behaviour that seeks to reject consumerism, rather, they are a descriptive one in which the aim is to be specific about the criteria, in this case the price, of what is consumed. This means that the decision regarding what *izikhothane* buy is mainly influenced by the object's ability to communicate a message that is congruent with their desired identity. In contrast to the media narrative of *izikhothane* being representatives of moral decay, Howell and Vincent (2014: 62) comment that for these impoverished youths, conspicuous consumption becomes an avenue for enhancing their self-esteem within the context of limited opportunities. The same could possibly be achieved through socially desirable jobs, property, or even cars.

Further, participating in conspicuous consumption is articulated as a way of having fun in the face of the negativity that confronts young men in impoverished communities that are also ravaged by violent crimes. For *izikhothane*, in the presence of poverty and violence, 'having fun while you still can' is far more attractive than waiting for a future that may never come. This observation reminds me of the eloquently carved words by the food anthropologist Anna Trapido in her biography of Nelson Mandela, titled *Hunger for Freedom: The Story of Food in the Life of Nelson Mandela* (2008), where she narrates Mandela's and other defendants' engagement in parties and their way of 'living in the present' during the Rivonia Trial:

> Despite his domestic situation, Madiba joined in the mood of abundance and devil-may-care that took over many of the defendants. Though the state's case seemed weak, the death penalty was always a looming possibility and wild partying a common response of the defendants. Joe Slovo and Ruth

> First gave dance parties where everyone drank and jived the nights away. But, even getting drunk was not as simple as it might seem. George Bizos recollected: 'even for the unbanned people, you had to be a very quick drinker so that if there was a police raid, they only found empty glasses. Because it was illegal for black people to have intoxicating liquor, so we served short tots'. (Trapido 2008: 95)

Trapido's (2008) narration shows that amid atrocities and future uncertainties, pleasures that can be gleaned from the present may offer solace. Of course, the tendency to live in the present is criticised by writers who label contemporary youth as the 'lost generation' and accuse them of wasting themselves because they have lost interest in politics (Richards & Langa 2018: 87). Granted, it would be absurd to compare the strife of the Rivonia Trialists to that of *izikhothane*; their struggles, goals and aspirations are certainly different. Nonetheless, all people seek ways to deal with uncertainties. Living in the present seems to provide a space to locate the self, albeit momentarily, in sanity and stability, to appreciate that moment which is certain and known, unlike the mysterious and unknown tomorrow. In these two instances – the Rivonia Trial and *ukukhothana* – wild partying seemingly fulfils the participants.

Howell and Vincent (2014) comment on *ukukhothana*'s constant reiteration of heteronormative gender relations, particularly the tendency characteristic of patriarchy, to frame women as subservient to the interests of men. In the case of *izikhothane*, girlfriends are often treated as trophies that symbolise victory. *Izikhothane* treats women as their possessions to be protected from other crews; the protection is not from violence but rather from being lured by a rival crew. When girls are involved in *ukukhothana*, they form a circle around the 'dissing' battles to scream and cheer for the boys (Howell & Vincent 2014; Jones 2013; Mkhwanazi 2011). The presence of girls, especially those considered beautiful, adds to the credibility of the crew.

To ensure completeness or wholeness, a crew of *izikhothane* should have a combination of expensive clothes; alcohol, including expensive spirits or whiskey; girls; a taxi with loud music and the name of the crew written on the windows of the taxi using white wax polish. They should host parties, dance, 'diss' each other and destroy their costly possession (Howell & Vincent 2014: 69). According to Howell and Vincent (2014), for many black township males, the pursuit of citizenship in the new South Africa is associated with being an object of respect amid inequality and persistent poverty, which can only be garnered through conspicuous consumption. This is evident from the often-cited role models such as 'Sushi King', Kenny Kunene. There is dissonance between the dreams of *izikhothane* and the reality that confronts them.

Consumption leaves no vacuum: The contextual consumption of izikhothane

Izikhothane come from communities; they do not exist in a vacuum. Their actions are connected to their communities' history, present and future. This perspective is espoused by Koyi Mchunu (2016) in '*Izikhothane* Youth Phenomenon: The Janus Face of Contemporary Culture in South Africa'. Similar to other studies of *ukukhothana*, Mchunu's (2016) study is informed by a constructionist paradigm that seeks to probe the subculture by looking at it through the eyes of its adherents to understand how they make sense of the world. Mchunu argues that *izikhothane*, similar to the rest of South African society, are trying to locate themselves in a post-apartheid context characterised by consumerism. For Mchunu (2016), subcultures such as *ukukhothana* are offshoots of dominant cultures and represent an extreme version of these dominant cultures in our society.

Mchunu's (2016) paper suggests a correlation between engaging in society through, for example, studying or being employed and participating in the *ukukhothana* subculture. He found that 40 per cent of the participants in his study had completed Matric, out of which only 10 furthered their studies at tertiary level, while an astonishing 60 per cent had dropped out at various school levels. Mchunu's participants were unwilling to disclose how they funded their participation in the subculture. Instead, they used sweeping statements such as 'I am a hustler', which has to do with one doing anything to fund a lifestyle and make a living. Some said they were employed, yet they did not specify their line of employment. Mchunu (2016) notes that in explaining their purpose for participating in *ukukhothana*, the participants spoke about having fun because they are still young, while others pointed to being inspired by older and more prominent members of society whose luxurious lifestyles they admired.

Further, Mchunu (2016) sees the preoccupation with materialism in the form of expensive clothes and alcohol and their destruction as representative of the Janus face of contemporary South Africa in which the youth try to find meaning and place amid blocked aspirations. According to Mchunu (2016: 7), '*izikhothane* represent a tragicomic dramatization of the pervasive culture of spectacle as embedded in new forms of architecture, the emerging geographies of retailing and consumption, and the ubiquitous lavish display of an enticing array of consumer products'. As a result, the apparent dissonance in the dichotomy of reality and imagination played out in the subculture of *ukukhothana* has evoked discussions about rethinking the idea of resistance.

Expressing desire through resistance

The known reality within which *izikhothane* live is one of poverty and relative scarcity, which is subverted through consumption. This necessitates a conversation around a special kind of resistance, a kind that is not necessarily orchestrated with the intention of refusing something, but rather one that speaks to deep desires for something. Alice Inggs (2017) discusses this view in her journal article titled 'The Suit is Mine: *Skhothane* and the Aesthetic of the African Modern'. Inngs (2017: 92) remarks that '*izikhothane* do not represent a form of resistance to the hegemony of wider society and its values, but rather a hyperbolic exaggeration of these values as advertised by mainstream media and venerated on social media: wealth, celebrity, visibility'. The upward mobility that *izikhothane* perform, which is financed through working class efforts, is supposedly superficial because wealth is secondary to the performance of wealth, which implies an orchestrated act (Inggs 2017). Though *izikhothane* are often referred to as a subculture (Howell & Vincent 2014; Jones 2013), for Inngs (2017) they are different from Dick Hebdige's (1979) classical countercultural meaning of the term 'subculture'.

ACADEMIC PERSPECTIVES ON *UKUKHOTHANA*

Izikhothane represent a complex performative aesthetic formed in response to the township space and provide a contribution to the emerging aesthetic of metropolitan modernity in post-apartheid South Africa. Inggs (2017: 94) notes that *izikhothane* also represent an underground youth culture that resists easy categorisations and works against a present in which unemployment is a reality. *Izikhothanes*' subversive resistance to undesirable conditions of impoverishment gives 'voice to imaginative worlds very different from those of the parental generation' (Nuttall in Inggs 2017: 94). Given the complexity of spectacle that characterises *ukukhothana* and the imaginative superficiality of the subculture, Inggs (2017: 96) draws parallels to Mikhail Bakhtin's (1984) carnivalesque.

The carnivalesque is a 'linguistic and embodied social practice that degrades culturally rarefied discourses by transferring these texts, which speak in the language of the high, spatial, and abstract to their material grounding in the bodily lower stratum' (Bakhtin 1984: 19). During the carnivalesque, the world is briefly transformed through the subversion of social norms; the lines of distinction between superior and inferior, master and subject, moral and immoral, are blurred without punishment or consequence (Lewis & Piles 1996). Inggs (2017) argues that in the 'superficial' subculture of *ukukhothana*, the distinguishing lines between rich and poor are erased. This results in the simultaneous creation of a link between spaces of affluence and modernity and zones of poverty. Like the carnivalesque, during *izikhothane*'s events, sacrilegious acts of destruction, including money burning, are licensed and not punished. The mock battles embody a protest aspect inherent in the carnivalesque against economic impoverishment that suggests a subtle social resistance (Inggs 2017).

This type of subtle resistance and protest are further discussed by Carl Death, a senior lecturer of international political economy in the Department of Politics at the University of Manchester, who in 2016 published an article titled 'Counter-conducts as a Mode of Resistance: Ways of "Not Being Like That" in South Africa'. Death (2016) discusses *ukukhothana* in Soweto as reminiscent of a social movement. He examines this subculture through the 'counter-conducts' approach, which draws its inspiration from the work of Michel Foucault to offer a nuanced understanding of resistance. Death (2016: 202) argues that the 'counter-conducts approach can draw attention to modes of protest which form in parallel to techniques of governmentality; are deeply interpenetrated with the power relations they oppose; and which facilitate or enable the production and performance of alternative subjectivities through processes of ethical self-reflection: ways of not being like that'.

The counter-conducts approach provides an opportunity to dissect the concept of resistance to show how resistance practices can subvert dominant ways of being (Death 2010, 2016). The approach opens a space where those who participate in *ukukhothana* can be observed from a perspective that acknowledges their voice in seeking to be understood outside the confines of poor victims and perceived instead as active dreamers. In this sense, the behaviour of *izikhothane* should be read from a perspective that accepts that their impoverishment is not all that they are. They are not just victims of circumstance but individuals with a sense of agency and direction who are deliberate in their actions. The 'waste' perceived in their actions is not an end but a means to communicate an identity that transcends the confines of poverty. The aim is to resist hegemonic classifications of social class by conducting themselves in a manner that is counter to societal expectations and communicate the message that 'we are not like that' (Death 2016).

Ukukhothana *in modern spaces*

An element of the subculture of *ukukhothana* that is not always given much attention is that of aesthetics and artwork. In 2016, in her Visual Arts master's thesis submitted to the University of South Africa titled 'Dedicated to Society's Misunderstood, Those That are Often Defined as "Weird", "Shocking" or Just "Unusual"', Nkosikhona Ngcobo 'explores the representation of *s'khothane* in selected contemporary visual artworks and assesses any influence it might have on these artworks' (Ngcobo 2016: iv). For the project, Ngcobo randomly selected events that took place in recreational parks, such as Fountains Valley in Tshwane, at taverns in Soshanguve, and in Thembisa. Ngcobo (2016:

iv) argues that the subculture of *ukukhothana* is 'widely integrated and visually appropriated in the visual language of selected contemporary South African art practices'. Amid the chastising narrative that is embedded in media representations of *izikhothane* and public discourses about the subculture, Ngcobo (2016) observes that artistic representations of this subculture are devoid of any embodiment of explicit judgement. Ngcobo concludes that *ukukhothana* is embedded in the South African pop culture landscape in a unique manner that is always overlooked by investigative journalistic accounts. Further, *ukukhothana* is influential in contemporary visual arts practices. It provides a source of psychological well-being and is a vehicle through which to respond to social challenges that confront the youth in post-apartheid South Africa (Ngcobo 2016: 97).

Busisiwe Memela's (2018) Master of Applied Arts in Fashion submitted at the Durban University of Technology offers a fascinating perspective on *ukukhothana*, by identifying *izikhothane* as a neo-tribe. Memela worked with a crew of *izikhothane* called The Italian Gates and argues that to label *ukukhothana* as a subculture is extensively limiting and fails to consider the nuances of identity formation and identity expressions in the postmodern society. As a result, she opts to use the concept of neo-tribes to classify *izikhothane* as a postmodern style community (Memela 2018: 55).

Memela's study aims to uncover the stylistic nuances of the *s'khothane* neo-tribe and map out the factors that inform the use of fashion in the project of identity expression. She relies on phenomenological epistemology and ethnographic methods to collect data. The theoretical underpinnings of the study (Memela 2018: 3) are rooted in 'post-subculture theory with the underlying themes of self-reflexivity, cultural capital and neo-tribes'. As such, Memela (2018: 103) reports that The Italian Gates can be conceived as being 'intertextual authors in their use of luxury clothes to portray the image of their desired affluence and social positions'. Viewed from this perspective, the emergence of the neo-tribe reaffirms the postmodern reality; more so, it demonstrates a shift in the identities of young black South Africans.

Memela's (2018: 103) study reveals that the media has sensationalised and perpetuated the notion of vandalism and destruction, which has come to be known as characteristic of *ukukhothana*. Similarly, Richards found in his 2015 study of *izikhothane* in Katlehong that their practice of destruction is generally influenced by media sensationalism and is not necessarily ubiquitous. Effectively, a reductive and sensationalist representation of the phenomenon as solely destructive fails to consider all other aspects of the subculture.

Memela's positioning of *ukukhothana* within the discourses of a postmodern society calls for us to rethink our readings of this phenomenon as a subculture. The concept of subculture conjures up images of resistance, oversimplifies *ukukhothana* and detracts from the complex nature of consumption in post-apartheid South Africa.

Izikhothane: *Are they a subculture?*

Most accounts of *ukukhothana* label it as a subculture (see Jones 2013; Mkhwanazi 2011; Mnisi 2015; Richards 2015; Richards & Langa 2018; Howell & Vincent 2014). However, two accounts dispute this classification as simplistic. On the one hand, Inggs (2017: 90) positions *ukukhothana* 'not so much as a subculture but rather as a performative aesthetic existing in a continuum of styles'. On the other hand, Memela (2018) discusses *ukukhothana* from a post-subcultural theory perspective as a neo-tribe in a post-modern society. To address the question of how to conceptualise *ukukhothana*, I first discuss the concept of subculture epistemologically, then I contextualise it within this book.

The concept of subculture is not without contestation, particularly as a Western concept. Hence, it is fitting to problematise it within the post-apartheid South African context. The term itself has a negative connotation because it is largely associated with ideas of aggression, deviance, division and subgroups. My aim is not to redefine the concept of subculture but to operationalise it so that it serves the purpose of making sense of *izikhothane* behaviour.

Theories of subculture build on the work of the American-born sociologist Robert Merton's (1938) 'strain theory', which posits that subcultures emerge as individuals' efforts to adapt to the strain they experience in their environment. Often, the adaptation takes the form of delinquency, which is violent and malicious. Although Merton (1938) acknowledges that such delinquency is present across various class structures, he focuses predominantly on working-class males.

According to Merton (1938: 672), 'certain phases of social structure generate the circumstances in which the infringement of social codes constitutes a normal response'. Merton suggests that acts of delinquency perpetrated by members of a subculture are aimed at acquisitive crime. He identifies two major elements or phases of social and cultural structures that are sources of deviant behaviour: cultural goals and institutional norms. The first social structure phase consists of culturally defined goals, purposes, and interests; it comprises the frame of aspirational reference (Merton 1938: 672). The second phase defines, regulates, and controls the acceptable modes of achieving certain cultural aspirations and goals. Any conduct that deviates from the cultural goals and the methods of achieving these goals that may appear to be outside the defined modes is considered deviant.

Much of the later subcultural theory came from work conducted at the University of Birmingham's Centre for Contemporary Cultural Studies (CCCS), established in 1964 (Gelder & Thornton 1997). The Birmingham school linked subcultures to youths from working-class backgrounds who resisted perceived class-related problems. The CCCS's conceptions of youth subcultures were primarily based on social class resistance and on working-class youth attempting to make sense of themselves in a society that relegates them to marginality. In subsequent years, CCCS's subculture theory attracted extensive criticism for being Eurocentric. Further, the CCCS was criticised for failing to consider the formation of race and ethnic subcultures (Jensen 2011: 4). Discomfort with the subcultural theory gave birth to the post-subculture paradigm.

Post-subcultural theory emerged and gained traction in youth studies from the early 1990s to the new millennium. The term 'post-subculture' was first used by Steve Redhead in his book titled *The End of the Century Party: Youth and Pop Towards 2000*, which was published in

1990. The book attempted to make sense of recurrent claims regarding the end of the 1980s conformist youth culture. The proponents of post-subcultural theory argue that the concept of subculture has become redundant in the context of a post-modern society in which 'youth identities are more flexible, fluid and fragmented due to the increasing flow of cultural commodities, images and texts through which more individualised identity projects and notions of self could be fashioned' (Bennett 1999: 493). The new perspective on youth cultural studies offered by post-subculture theory has indeed contributed significantly towards the understanding of youths and their appropriation processes of music, style, images and texts (Bennett 1999). This paradigm has already given rise to new concepts to explain youth groupings. Memela (2015) uses it in her study of *izikhothane*, which she describes as a neo-tribe. Bennett (1999: 599–600) opines that neo-tribes could be understood as 'temporal gatherings characterised by fluid boundaries and floating membership'. Central to this description is the postulation that coherence within a youth grouping is not necessarily the glue that keeps the group together but rather a common interest in music, style and dance. Post-subcultural theory postulates that the postmodern society is complex, and youth identities are in a state of flux. At the centre of the theory of post-subculture is the move away from cohesive youth groupings linked by a single style to a proliferation of many styles and individualism, which is characteristic of post-modern societies. Post-subcultural theory has influenced youth cultural studies significantly and contributes to understanding the cultural dynamics that inform how young people appropriate music, style, objects and texts (Bennett 1999: 492).

However, this paradigm has also attracted significant criticism. Despite the contribution that post-subcultural theory has made to youth studies, Bennett (1999: 494) notes that this paradigm has not necessarily replaced subcultural theory as an approach to youth research. Bennett offers a brief discussion of the shortfalls of the post-subculture theory. First, Bennett raises a concern about its novelty and argues that it remains theoretically loose and does not offer a concept enabling researchers to analyse youth culture. Second, the theory disregards class as the basis for forming youth identities in postmodern societies.

This is a problematic assumption because structural inequalities continue to shape youths' cultural options and affiliations (Bennett 1999: 494). Third, the tendency of post-subculture theory to emphasise reflexive individuality inadvertently depoliticises youth [culture.] Finally, the emphasis on the fluidity of urban youth cultures inherent to post-subculture theory overlooks some urban cultures that do not conform to this fluidity.

In this present book, considering the varied nature of *ukukhothana*, a view that homogenises it would undoubtedly yield analysis that is too limited to be reliable. Many of the shortfalls of the concept of subculture identified in post-subculture theory, in fact, justify my position in using the term. Concerning The Good Fellas, class struggles, spatial location, group structure, and discursive resistance continue to remain central to the group, thus rendering the subculture concept relevant. *Izikhothane* do not form a homogenous grouping. Therefore, the reference to them as either a subculture, as most other academics cited thus far have done, or as a 'neo-tribe' as Memela (2015) does, or a 'performative aesthetic' as posited by Inggs (2017), is dependent on the context in which one is studying them.

The organised nature of The Good Fellas and their tendency to enact an internal social hierarchy is characteristic of subcultures. Generally, subcultures are defiant in nature, and the same defiance works both as a social lubricant that brings them together and as a social glue that keeps them together. The tendency of *izikhothane* to engage in destruction goes against societal cultural norms of consumption, particularly in circumstances of economic deprivation. Like other subcultures, *izikhothane* have their own cultural code and values around fashion, sexuality and aspirations. However, they are unique in the sense that their resistance and defiance are of a symbolic and performative nature because they reject associations with poverty through the destruction of items of wealth. In this sense, they symbolically deviate from the poverty that confronts them by portraying wealth that does not exist in real terms. Further, I choose the concept of subculture because it allows me to focus on a small group of people who intentionally and deliberately organise themselves to behave in a different manner from their broader society to the extent that they embrace behaviour that is frowned upon by outsiders. These observable traits in *ukukhothana* are characteristic of subcultural behaviour. In addition, the concept of subculture enables one to study a unit of society in isolation and to focus on a group of people who are misunderstood due to their behaviour.

Hebdige (1979: 90) goes beyond deviance in making sense of subcultures and speaks about how they represent 'noise as opposed to sound'. A simple definition of noise is 'anything that interferes with the encoding, conveying or decoding of a message' (Du Plooy-Cilliers & Louw 2015: 6). Subcultures usually cause a disruption of the norm. This disruption happens because subcultures 'breach our expectancies' as they 'represent symbolic challenges to a symbolic order' (Hebdige 1979: 90). There is no doubt that *izikhothane* are 'noisy'. They have created a subculture through their unusual clothes and colour choices, their destruction of items of value, and their flamboyant dance moves intentionally choreographed to draw attention to their costly apparel, against the backdrop of poverty.

Subcultures cannot be ignored indefinitely because their noise elicits silencing or acknowledgement by the larger society. This happens through a process of incorporation, which often comes in two forms (Hebdige 1979). The first form involves the commodification of the signs of a subculture into mass-produced objects (Hebdige 1979: 95). Examples include the subcultural signs of clothes and music, which eventually find their market. In the case of *izikhothane*, it is evident that their dance moves have inspired music production and styles of dress outside the subculture itself. The second form of incorporating a subculture is the ideological form, which involves attempts by dominant social groups to position the subculture ideologically by attaching labels to it and redefining the behaviour that they consider to be deviant (Hebdige 1979: 96). An ideal example of the ideological form of incorporation by dominant groups in society is what scholars (including myself) have been doing through research. The attempt has been to make sense of the subculture of *izikhothane* by labelling it differently and redefining the deviance in various ways. Once we get to a point where we have established a fair understanding of the subculture, the 'noise' caused by it is contextualised and repositioned because of interpretation. It is in this context that I use the concept of subculture.

Note

1   Moganedi K (2015) Sushi king: I bonked them!. *Daily Sun*, 25 May. https://www.dailysun.co.za/News/Entertainment/Sushi-king-I-bonked-the20150525

3 Consumption, masculinities and izikhothane

Although theories enable us to make sense of phenomena, they often fall short of accounting for everything relating to a single phenomenon. It would be difficult, if not impossible, to have a grand theory of consumption that explains *ukukhothana* in every context because of the multifaceted complexities of its manifestations. In this book, the focus is on understanding the relationship between consumption practised in *ukukhothana* and the resultant performance and articulations of masculinities. Therefore, to make sense of *ukukhothana*, I draw from studies in the fields of masculinities, consumption and social psychology. Here, I discuss various accounts of consumption and masculinities, to provide a comprehensive framework within which to explore the subculture of *ukukhothana*. In this context, I discuss, first, the complex nature of consumption in the twenty-first century and, second, the idea of masculinities as it manifests in consumption in various contexts.

In the twenty-first century, studying peoples' consumption patterns is a complex undertaking because, on the one hand, consumption is influenced by economics, and on the other hand, it is shaped by social factors. When considering the economics of consumption, we must consider the interplay between the two market forces of demand and supply. However, when we look at the social aspect of consumption, we need to transcend the rational conclusions that can be drawn from the interpretations of demand and supply because other forces come into play. The focus is on the social aspect of consumption, which is linked to the economic aspect but transcends the rationale we may draw from it. I am fascinated by the violation of the basic law of economics. According to the basic economic law of demand and supply, if the prices of goods increase, the demand for them will decrease (Kugan 2019); as such, there is an inverse relationship between the price and the quantity demanded of a product. However, two types of goods violate the law of demand and supply: Giffen goods and Veblen goods.

Sir Robert Giffen, after whom the Giffen good is named, observed that the demand for this type of good increases as its price increases and falls when the price drops (Kenton 2019). While some scholars argue that Giffen goods do not exist (Baruch & Kannai 2001; Kohli 1986), scholars such as Nachbar (1998) have identified them. Doi, Iwasa and Shimomura (2009: 248) argue that 'Giffen goods demonstrate a behaviour which is independent of wealth level and is often exhibited by households that have low real levels of wealth'. These goods depend on context, influenced by location and society, as they tend to be unique to these. Giffen goods mostly include low-income, non-luxury goods that may be staple foods within given societies or other products that cannot be easily substituted. For example, maize meal could be a Giffen good in South Africa because, regardless of its price increase, most people – especially households with lower levels of income – will continue to buy it and spend less on other things such as meat, because it forms part of their staple diet (Chisholm 2018).

The Giffen good suggests that when prices rise, consumers are more likely to spend on products that form part of their staple diet, for which there are no readily available cheaper substitutes. Since other products are more expensive, low-income consumers will likely direct their spending towards the Giffen good, which serves their primary needs, rather than a more expensive alternative. The consumption of this Giffen good then becomes the focus of much of the expenditure of the low-income household. Therefore, consumption of Giffen goods increases, relative to other goods, when prices increase. For example, if the price of maize meal increases, poor households will likely divert more money towards buying it because it is a necessity. Expenditure on meat and other more expensive goods will decline with the decline in the households' disposable income resulting from the rise in the price of maize meal.

Another good that violates the basic law of demand and supply is the Veblen good, also a type of commodity for which the demand increases as the price increases (Arronson & Johansson-Stenman 2012). Thorstein Veblen, an American economist and sociologist, was one of the earliest writers to analyse consumption behaviour in America. In his seminal book *The Theory of the Leisure Class* (1899), a critique of the nineteenth-century American consumer society, Veblen extensively discusses the relationship between status and consumption. He describes a kind of consumption characterised by goods that symbolise wealth, often dubbed in economics as the 'Veblen effect' – hence the term 'Veblen goods' (Dolfsma 2000). Veblen goods are used as markers of social status because, as products of superior quality, they suggest wealth (Pettinger 2017) and are sought after by most people within an economy or society. In this sense, a Veblen good is the kind of good whose demand tends to increase with an increase in its price. An example of a Veblen good could include a luxury car such as a BMW. This is pertinent because the behaviour of *izikhothane* seems to defy what could be considered rational and seems to contradict the logic of the demand and supply curve. Several scholars who have studied this contradictory behaviour observe that poor people demand visibly expensive goods regardless of the high prices and their low income (Banerjee & Duflo 2007; Kaus 2010; Moav & Neeman 2010, 2012).

Veblen's work (1899/2003) suggests a correlation between consumption behaviour, socioeconomic status and identity. He examines the extent to which the need for personal recognition, which to him translates as honour, rests on the public display of material acquisition. In this chapter, I will look at the study of consumption with a particular focus on Veblen's idea of 'conspicuous consumption' and its relevance to South Africa in the twenty-first century.

The Theory of the Leisure Class was first published while Veblen worked at the University of Chicago. It was written amid precarious economic and social upheavals in the United States of America due to rapid industrialisation that led to the growth of industries such as coal mining and steel production. Veblen (1899/2003) particularly focused on the elite distinction that was evident during this time. An increase in the number of mines, coupled with the construction of factories and railroads, resulted in gargantuan fortunes for the men who were involved in this industrialisation as owners (Posel & Van Wyk 2019: 5). The last three decades of the nineteenth century led to an upsurge of multimillionaires whose lives ostentatiously evidenced their success.

This is the era in which industrialists like Andrew Carnegie, John D. Rockefeller, Solomon Guggenheim and many others flourished. Economic and social inequality in the United States was rapidly increasing, with greater proportions of Americans becoming poor. The wealthy founded their own elite schools and private clubs and lived in mansions with rare artworks and well-dressed servants (Posel & van Wyk 2019: 5).

Veblen coined the phrase 'conspicuous consumption' to explain the purchase of certain goods not for their utility value but to distinguish oneself from others as having superior wealth and higher social standing. Conspicuous consumption, also known as the 'Veblen effect', refers to the purchase of expensive luxury goods with an equivalent if not lower functional value compared to less costly counterparts (Charoenrook & Thakor 2008). A conspicuous item is thus an item that is consumed primarily for its ability to bestow a high social status on an individual (Charoenrook & Thakor 2015). This means that the social signalling aspects of a product precede its utility value. Such goods are luxurious because, first, those who consume them can live without them. Second, they are not bought with the sole aim of aiding the performance of a certain task or function, as a cheaper counterpart can perform the same task or function. Third, these goods are utilised primarily for their social significance in relation to a reference group. In Veblen's time, people engaged in conspicuous consumption to show that they were wealthy. Veblen (1899/2003) explained that to merely possess wealth is not enough to get respect and esteem; one must show wealth. The best way to do this is to engage in the kind of consumption that will signal wealth. For Veblen, conspicuous consumption was reserved for the members of the leisure class.

Veblen observed that the institution of the leisure class was visible at the height of the barbarian cultures such as feudal Europe and feudal Japan.[1,2] It was visible in such communities because class distinction was based on occupation. The upper classes were by custom exempt from industrial occupations and reserved for certain employments with a certain degree of honour attached to them (Veblen 1899/2003: 1). Chief among the honourable employments was warfare, with priestly services second. However, where warfare was not prominent or the community was not warlike, priestly services became a priority (Veblen 1899/2003: 1).

Occupation is, thus, a form of class distinction. Though Veblen notes that the importance of not working is a significant element of leisure class membership, he cautions that habitual neglect of work does not constitute a leisure class. At the centre of the definition of the leisure class is the idea of distinction from those stationed below in the class hierarchy. The leisure class lives off the fruits of the toil of the working class. Concerning the American leisure class, Veblen notes the importance of conspicuous leisure demonstrated by participating in sports, which suggests not working, and the exaggerated and elaborate dresses worn by the wives of the wealthy, which even hindered movement. These were among the markers of wealth that distinguished the leisure class from the working class.

The underlying assumption of Veblen's thesis is that conspicuous consumption is aimed at signalling wealth to others, enabling those who engage in it to gain a high social status. In this sense, conspicuous consumption distinguishes the leisure class from the lower classes, who merely emulate them in their consumption, albeit with cheaper versions.

The emulation model of conspicuous consumption

The concept of imitation was applied in fashion by the German sociologist George Simmel in *Fashion*, which was originally published in 1904. Simmel was one of the earliest writers to offer a theoretical framework in fashion (Maldini & Manz 2017). In his article, Simmel states:

> Fashion is a form of imitation and so of social equalization, but, paradoxically, in changing incessantly, it differentiates one time from another and one social stratum from another. It unites those of a social class and segregates them from others. The elite initiates a fashion and, when the mass imitates it in an effort to obliterate the external distinctions

of class, abandons it for a newer mode – a process that quickens with the increase of wealth. Fashion does not exist in tribal and classless societies. (Simmel 1904: 541)

Simmel contends that the social fact about fashion is that it derives from a basic tension that is specific to the human social condition. On the one end of the spectrum, some people have the inclination to imitate other people, while on the other end, there are people who have the impulse to distinguish themselves from others. This claim, which Simmel attributes to human nature, suggests that some people tend to imitate whom they admire, while others aim to distinguish themselves from those towards whom they are indifferent, or they despise and perceive to be inferior (Benvenuto 2000). By this, Simmel implies that fashion does not exist in classless societies, meaning that it is the poor or those without wealth who admire and imitate the wealthy.

Though Simmel uses fashion to make a point about imitation, he comments more broadly on the ordering of social life, which he divides into two symmetries: the 'haves', who elicit admiration and distinguish themselves through their consumption and fashion choice, versus the 'have-nots', who admire and imitate their economic superiors. According to this principle, fashion is both a product of class distinction (Pyyhtinen 2018) and also works to distinguish the upper classes from the lower classes. '[F]or fashion to exist, society must be stratified, some members must be perceived as inferior or superior – or simply as worthy or unworthy of being imitated' (Benvenuto 2000: 3). If the lower classes seek to imitate the upper classes, the market will cater for this by providing a cheaper version of the fashion that is consumed by the upper classes (Currod-Halkett 2017). Once the lower classes' consumption of cheaper fashion items blurs the distinction, the upper classes begin to search for other fashion items that will again bring the lines of distinction into focus.

It should be noted that while Simmel used the concept of imitation extensively in relation to fashion, it was the French sociologist, criminologist and psychologist Gabriel Tarde (1843–1904) who first conceived the concept of imitation. Tarde (1903) noted that sociology is based on psychological interactions among individuals with the fundamental forces rooted in the laws of imitation and innovation (Djellal & Gallouj 2014). Drawing on Tarde's notion of imitation, Simmel was one of several European scholars who, at the turn of the twentieth century, devoted much of their attention to the analysis of elite distinction (though the topic was not necessarily new then). Some of these pioneers include the English sociologist Herbert Spencer who studied Victorian fashion, the German sociologist Max Weber, and the German economist and historian Werner Sombart who fell from fame because of his embrace of Nazism (Turner et al. 2002). They all made notable contributions to our understanding of the sociology of elite distinction.

This present book is especially indebted to Veblen (1899/2003) because of his direct focus on the role of consumption in social class distinction and status signalling and his reference to Simmel's emulation model to explain the notion of elite distinction through conspicuous consumption. The concept of conspicuous consumption, which typically refers to 'that which is judged extravagant, luxurious or wasteful' (Campbell 1995: 38), is presently widely used with reference to contemporary cultures where consumption is prevalent. It relates to the ways in which people seek to display and make visible to others their wealth, social position and status. Veblen (1899/2003: 85) pinpoints two ways in which individuals might demonstrate wealth through 'the element of waste' or wasteful activities: wasting time and effort by pursuing activities associated with leisure rather than work, often in ritualistic ways, such as sports; and squandering or wasting money on goods by lavish and excessive consumption.

Veblen points out that conspicuous consumption is a leading mechanism of social change. He proposes a framework in which people's preferences are understood to be established socially in relation to other people's positions in the social hierarchy (Sassatelli 2007). Following Simmel's (1904) notion of the 'trickle down' theory, subordinate groups, in keeping with the principle of imitation, set out to obtain new status and prestige by adopting expensive-looking clothing worn by members of the wealthy upper classes. The less wealthy seek to show off their 'elegant' attire, often cheaper versions, to convey the impression that they supposedly did not engage in manual labour or industrial work, and to imply that they too were members of the leisure society (Sassatelli 2007: 67–73; Veblen 1899/2003).

The 'trickle-down' effect noted by Simmel and Veblen in their emulation model has provided the basis for many studies of social distinction, social mobility and the hierarchical reproduction of taste in which the competition for status was perceived as central (Douglas & Isherwood 1979; McCracken 1988; Simmel 1904; Veblen 1899/2003). However, these notions have been interrogated and critiqued (see 1995; Maldini & Manz 2017; McCracken 1988; Sassatelli 2007). A leading criticism relates to the claim that Veblen's (1899/2003) model of emulation assumes that aspiring to emulate those stationed above one is a reductive, universal imperative; it does not consider the complexities involved in the selection of how specific social conduct might be imitated and creatively adapted in various complex ways and cultural contexts. As noted by Sassatelli (2007), Veblen believed that conspicuous consumption in industrial centres extends to entire populations, so the less wealthy, subordinate groups are concerned solely with imitating those socially superior to them.

This reductive view implies that less fortunate social groups can never generate their own fashions. Further, this view does not entirely account for how consumers or 'followers of fashion' frequently choose certain styled options over others. Crucially, even when people imitate their superiors, they always make selections and do not blindly emulate all available options. This means that certain options will be rejected in favour of other options that are taken up and modified (Sassatelli 2007: 68). For example, how *izikhothane* compile their outfits – incorporating an element of actively seeking attention and honour through performative acts – is unique to the subculture.

Furthermore, Veblen's model of emulation places envy at the centre of social motivations and does not consider more contemporary understandings of the culture of consumption, where identification and imitation are perceived to take place alongside more creative and selective procedures of reproduction (Sassatelli 2007: 69; see also Bourdieu 1984). In other words, the social history and cultural contexts of 'objects', their meanings and how they are used are also conditional on people's lives and the affordances and constraints thereof, and on people's personal or socially determined relationships with 'things' or objects (Cikszentmihalyi & Rochberg-Halton 1981).

Much criticism against the emulation model within consumer research in the last 50 years has focused on its inaccuracy, at least in relative contexts. Consumer research has indeed highlighted elite distinction yet sought to celebrate the individual as a 'self-made project' with the ability to choose what she or he wants and reject what she or he does not want. This opposes the idea of blind acceptance of consumption patterns of those stationed above (Baudrillard 1998; Firat & Venkatesh 1995). However, proponents of the emulation model argue that its opponents do not understand its fundamental tenets. These scholars cite examples from marketing research or reality television programmes such as 'MTV Cribs', 'The Millionaire Matchmaker', and 'Keeping up with the Kardashians' and urge a deeper understanding and more contextually nuanced applications of the emulation model (Maldini & Manz 2017). Indeed, previous research on *izikhothane* shows how they do not always sacrifice quality for cheaper versions of the brands that are consumed by the wealthy (Mnisi 2019). Considering how *izikhothane* creatively generate their own styles and fashions, which are not wholly modelled on those positioned above them in the social hierarchy, puts the relevance of the theory of emulation into question. This is because the theory makes no case for the complex creative networks of style and fashion consumption characterised by a plurality of options, views and perspectives. In fact, it does not aid in understanding how to conceptualise the consumption patterns of those considered marginal to Veblen's and Simmel's original theses. Though it is evident that *izikhothane* have role models who inspire them and whom they admire, the creativity that influences their style and subcultural practices is unlike anything that we have seen in post-apartheid South Africa (Richards & Langa 2018). This opens the debate about consumption even further, raising the question of why some consumption variants spark discussion while others do not. For example, the flames that engulf the costly apparel of the *izikhothane* spark controversy, while the conspicuous consumption of the elite and super-rich, even when considered unethical, produces little to no prolonged conversation and outrage.

Given the diluted nature of the emulation model and its inability, in contemporary times and locations, to effectively distinguish the wealthy from the poor, I find research on what has been dubbed the 'bottom of the pyramid' (BoP) consumer segment particularly pertinent to the study of conspicuous consumption in the context of poverty.[3] In the next section, I discuss work that has been done in the BoP segment to understand the arcane idea of supposedly poor people consuming beyond their means and what they can comfortably afford. These studies help provide a perspective and theoretical lens through which we can read *ukukhothana*.

Consumption of the consumer segment at the bottom of the pyramid

Surprisingly, *izikhothane* can finance their participation in this costly subculture. How does one make sense of a poor person who generally lacks access to necessities but affords to engage in conspicuous consumption? This could be accounted for by turning our attention to studies on an overlooked market – the bottom of the pyramid (BoP) consumer segment. Work done in this area informs us that there is potentially sufficient money among those considered poor, and we are simply unaware of it. A question immediately arises: why do we say the people in this segment are poor if they have money? This section of the chapter discusses the BoP consumer segment: those who are poor yet with significant buying power. In turn, this discussion can facilitate an understanding of *izikhothane*.

As will be evident, it is difficult to merge two research traditions, one from a business perspective and the other from a communication tradition. However, what makes this possible is that business research on the BoP segment has benefitted from employing qualitative inquiry methods, bringing it closer to the context and methodology of this book.

Much research suggests that poor people tend to engage in conspicuous consumption worldwide (Lamont & Molnar 2001; Banerjee & Duflo

2007; Moav & Neeman 2008; Charoenrook & Thakor 2008). Of interest is the segment of poor, BoP consumers, a socioeconomic concept used to group a vast segment of the world's poorest population living on less than $2 per day (CioIndex 2021). The phrase 'bottom of the pyramid' was first used by the former president of the United States of America, Franklin D. Roosevelt, during his radio address titled, 'The Forgotten Man' (Subhan & Khattak 2017: 1). During his 7 April 1932 address, Roosevelt remarked:

> These unhappy times call for the building of plans that rest upon the forgotten, the unorganized but the indispensable units of economic power, for plans like those of 1917 that build from the bottom up and not from the top down, that put their faith once more in the forgotten man at the bottom of the economic pyramid.

Roosevelt delivered this speech amid the Great Depression that lasted from 1929 to 1939. He was urging that those considered poor should be included in the work of rebuilding the economy.

Indian-born, University of Michigan distinguished professor Coimbatore Krishnarao Prahalad is credited for being the earliest scholar to study the BoP (2005, 2006, 2012). Prahalad (2005: 4) argues that the 'distribution of wealth and the capacity to generate income in the world can be captured as an economic pyramid. At the top of the pyramid are the wealthy, with numerous opportunities for generating high levels of income'. More than 4 billion people live at the BoP on less than $2 per day (Prahalad 2005: 4). There are ongoing debates around the BoP segment, mainly because of disagreements about the level of the poverty line, the number of people that are at the BoP, and the potential of the industry itself.

To provide insight into the BoP consumer, Subhan and Khattak (2017) argue that the BoP is an unexploited emerging market worth trillions of dollars, to be taken advantage of by global companies. Nicole (2003) adds that if companies want to tap into this huge market and gear towards servicing the BoP, they must reconfigure their business assumptions, models and practices. However, this emerging BoP market has not been significantly exploited because it is complex. Much reluctance stems from whether this huge segment of the population who earn approximately $2 per day can become profitable consumers for business, given that they struggle to make basic ends meet (Fosnacht 2013).

This complexity – which results from the market definition – is the focal point of much critique levelled at BoP research. Often, the concept of absolute poverty, which takes cognisance of a person's daily income, is used to define the BoP. The measure of absolute poverty is generally agreed to be earnings between $1 and $2 per day (Fosnacht 2013). However, purchasing power parity (PPP) can also be a useful measure of poverty. The PPP is a concept that serves two purposes. Firstly, it is used as the theory for the determination of exchange rates, which asserts that the change between two currencies over any period is determined by the change in the relative price levels of countries (Dornbusch 1985). The PPP is also used to measure people's living standards across countries (Lafrance & Schembri 2002). This means that the PPP is used to measure the price of a basket of identically traded goods and services in different countries, thereby providing a standardised indication of the standard of living (Prahalad 2005).

However, Kernani (2007) cautions that it is irrational to look at poverty solely in economic terms – through people's income or lack thereof – as other broader social, cultural and historical factors need to be considered. These factors may provide a more nuanced understanding of poverty and its persistence in some instances (Ramphoma 2014). However, considering the latter complicates understanding the BoP's boundaries. Prahalad's determination of BoP boundaries has been questioned; some disagree with him, primarily on the numbers that make up the BoP and its business potential. According to Prahalad (2005), its PPP is $13 trillion, but other researchers argue that although the earning potential is in the trillion-dollar region, $13 trillion is tremendously exaggerated (Kernani 2007; World Economic Forum 2009). The full extent of the earning potential of the BoP population segment for businesses and the subsequent contestations are not within the scope of this book; of importance is the consensus that the BoP exists and that people with incomes between $1 and $2 engage in conspicuous consumption (Gupta & Srivastav 2016; Kernani 2007; Prahalad, 2005; Prahalad & Hammond 2002; World Economic Forum 2009).

The rationale is that the BoP population segment can provide opportunities for global businesses to grow rapidly. Thus, businesses should focus on the supposedly 'forgotten man' (to borrow from Roosevelt), who is largely unserved due to his perceived unserviceability and unaffordability. There is a twofold motivation behind the studies of the BoP segment. First, these studies arise from efforts to alleviate poverty by integrating economically marginal people into the formal economy. Second, they arise from the perceived potential growth in companies' bottom lines when considering the aggregate purchasing power in a concentrated global market and its growth opportunity. Indeed, the potential for competitive business growth in the BoP market is well-established globally.

As much as this field of research has grown considerably in the last decade (Kolk et al. 2013), there remains a significant gap in the literature on this market segment at a country-specific level (Lappeman et al. 2019). This book seeks to provide insight on how this developing BoP theory could potentially enable an understanding of the consumption patterns of South African youths in this category. As such, the next section discusses the characteristics of the South African BoP market and how these characteristics relate to *izikhothane* as a subculture.

Characteristics of the South African market at the bottom of the pyramid

The BoP market is unique and specific to each country across the globe. Understanding and acknowledging this market aspect is important as it could reveal many traits of the population segment that would otherwise be ignored through homogenising people – a limitation in any research. An approach that considers heterogeneity is apposite. Here, I discuss characteristics identified by the University of Cape Town scholars James Lappeman, Kristin Ransome and Zach

Louw (2019) in a paper titled 'Not One Segment: Using Global and Local BoP Characteristics to Model Country-specific Consumer Profiles'. Lappeman et al. (2019) argue that a generic BoP segmentation strategy does not represent a multi-country BoP consumer profile. They discuss eight characteristics of BoP consumers that are common globally and add five specific to South Africa.

The first characteristic is significant buying power. Kotler and Armstrong (2015) explain that this refers to an individual's capacity to buy a certain quantity of goods and services. The BoP is often characterised by its high aggregated buying power. There is no consensus on the actual amount that denotes the buying power of the BoP, but it is estimated at around US$ 1.3 trillion (Lappeman et al. 2019). According to Nyanga (2015), the annual worth of the South African BoP is estimated at US$ 40.3 billion. This suggests that the South African BoP has a considerably high spending power in aggregate terms, despite low personal incomes (Lappeman et al. 2019: 321). The ability of *izikhothane* to raise money within their crew to hire a taxi and buy alcohol and clothes validates this buying power in aggregated terms.

Second, the lives of people who fall into the BoP segment are generally characterised by pressures exerted by poor infrastructure and economic constraints. Poor infrastructure is manifold and may encompass poor service delivery such as reliable electricity supply or proper housing. Economic constraints may include unemployment and underemployment, low and inconsistent incomes, and high inflation rates, which often hit the BoP segment quicker and harder than the middle class, thus impacting its consumption (Lappeman et al. 2019: 322). *Izikhothane* are mostly unemployed and often describe themselves as 'hustlers'. They are often colloquially described through the idiom of 'loxion management', which means 'making a plan' to survive in the township in the midst of urban unemployment (Mabena 2017: 7). Others are dependent on their working-class parents (Jones 2013; Mchunu 2016; Mkhwanazi 2011). Further, townships like Thembisa have been known to have many service delivery protests, including violent ones resulting in the arrest of some protestors (Mkhize 2014).[4]

Third, functional illiteracy affects those in the BoP segment. A person who is functionally illiterate has a basic education, but their reading and writing skills are not sufficient for everyday needs. They cannot use their ability to read, write or calculate to bring about development in their community (Vagvolyi et al. 2016: 1).

In South Africa, the rate of functional illiteracy is 78 per cent among Grade 4 learners, which means that the next generation of workers in the country will possibly enter the workforce without the necessary skills to elevate themselves out of poverty (Howie et al. 2017). This finding raises concerns about literacy and poverty alleviation in the country. However, Lappeman et al. (2019: 322) note that the relevance of *ukukhothana* is the 'BoP consumers' potential use of pictographic thinking while processing brand related information'. They further opine that functionally illiterate consumers tend to trade off economic value and convenience for goals that are congruent to their emotions. Lappeman et al. (2019) report that among the youth, South Africa has a substantial education problem, only 21 per cent of those in high school attain a matric certificate. This concurs with Mchunu's (2016) study of *izikhothane*, in which 60 per cent of participants had dropped out of school with only 10 per cent being privileged enough to access tertiary education. Lappeman et al. (2019) report that over 50 per cent of South African learners who start Grade 1 drop out before completing their senior certificate. This is something that Mchunu also discovered in his study of *izikhothane*. The issue of poor academic performance has been reported in several studies of *izikhothane* (Jones 2013; Howell & Vincent, 2014; Mkwanazi 2011; Mnisi 2015).

Fourth, consumers are brand conscious when they seek to buy popular rather than lesser-known brands (Kotler & Armstrong 2015). Lappeman et al. (2019: 324) note that BoP consumers prefer goods that are branded as they provide backing, confidence and quality. In line with this observation, Prahalad and Hart (2002) argue that brand consciousness is ubiquitous among BoP consumers. In her 2015 Master of Business Administration thesis, titled 'The Nature of Brand Loyalty at the Base of the Pyramid', Memory Nyanga argues that South African BoP consumers are brand conscious and claim to buy many brands that they see on various media (Nyanga 2015: 66). As Prahalad (2012) explains, this is partly fuelled by the flooding of the BoP consumer segment with mediated marketing messages. Brand consciousness, particularly the hunger for popular consumer brands that often cost a lot and carry a higher social premium, is intensified by income inequality in South Africa (Ger & Belk 1996). *Izikhothane* seek premium brands and consume expensively, thus their consumption is termed conspicuous. Mkwanazi (2011) notes that they consciously seek expensive brands and deliberately reject cheap clothes, which fail to signal wealth in social interactions. Their hunger for costly branded consumer goods is partly linked to their sense of self.

Fifth, poverty is experienced as dehumanising and degrading by those who are at the bottom of the wealth pyramid, consequently, they perceive themselves as second-class citizens (Lappeman et al. 2019). In South Africa, this is often linked to the apartheid regime and its legacy. The apartheid system treated non-white people as second-class citizens to the extent that consumption was racialised. BoP consumers are concerned about maintaining self-respect and dignity (Lappeman et al. 2019). The consumers in this segment believe that the ability to accumulate material goods fosters self-esteem and positions them on par with the rest of society, at least at a symbolic level (Lappeman et al., 2019). Gupta and Srivastav (2015) link this tendency to the idea of the aspirations of poor consumers. *Izikhothane* generally feel empowered and more confident when they dress elegantly and expensively. While the literature fails to explain the link between the aspirations of BoP consumers and their motivation for engaging in costly expenditure, particularly in the South African context (Lappeman et al. 2019), the theme of pursuing dignity and honour through conspicuous consumption is present in most studies of *izikhothane*.

Sixth, consumers at the bottom of the pyramid tend to exhibit characteristics of companionship and social closeness. This segment of the population believes in partnership and social embeddedness when it comes to financial interactions and social interactions, as well as in understanding one another (Lappeman et al. 2019). Further, a collective mindset, shaped by shared experience, explains why BoP consumers desire to be like the rest of society: to consume like the middle class or even the wealthy. A spirit of comradery characterises *izikhothane*, evidenced in their tendency to help each other financially within the group through efforts such as establishing a common purse, which becomes useful when they need to buy clothes or attend events (Mnisi 2015).

Seventh, BoP consumers in developing countries have leapfrogged into the information age, characterised by a rapid uptake of mobile communication technologies. This has allowed them to take advantage of the devices and information that connect them. Lappeman et al. (2019) posit that the ownership of mobile phones in South Africa is over 75 per cent, most of which use prepaid sim cards. Having spent several years with various groups of *izikhothane*, I have yet to see a crew whose members do not have at least basic smartphones with internet access and are not active on social media networks such as Facebook, WhatsApp and Instagram. Vincent and Howell (2014) comment on how *izikhothane* use mobile phones to market their events and performances. In fact, most of the video footage that has caught the attention of media reportage was taken using cellular phones and posted on social media by *izikhothane*.

The final and eighth global characteristic of BoP consumers is that they do not trust large firms and their brands. However, whether this assumption applies to South African BoP consumers is unclear and requires further research (Lappeman et al. 2019). In fact, if this characteristic is accepted, it immediately contradicts the evident big brand consciousness, which is characteristic of *izikhothane*.

The next five points related to BoP consumers are unique to the South African context.

First, South Africa is a mix of first- and third-world economies with vibrant formal and informal business sectors (Simpson & Lappeman 2017). That is to say, South Africa is a hybrid economy – made up of the formal economy, with mostly registered and tax-paying businesses, as well as an informal sector characterised by small and typically unregistered businesses that do not pay business tax. Unfortunately, such a hybrid economy leads to an evident gap between the rich and the poor. The Gini coefficient, 'a statistical measure of the degree of dispersion intended to represent the income or wealth distribution of a nation's residents' (Lappeman et al. 2019: 325) rates South Africa as the most unequal country globally. The inequality in South Africa is pervasive and easily noticeable; for example, some middle- and upper-class 'leafy' suburbs are physically separated from the informal settlements by a road. In townships like Thembisa, where *ubukhothane* is practised, informal settlements are next to the more affluent bond/mortgage houses.

Second, income stability is characteristic of the South African context. Regardless of the low amount, there are more than 27 million beneficiaries of the South African Social Security Agency (SASSA 2023) social grant scheme, which accounts for about 45 per cent of the population. Child grants, disability grants, and pension grants boost the household income of BoP consumers (Lappeman et al. 2019). Dependency on social grants is common among some *izikhothane*, who might come from single-parent households or child-headed households or live with pensioner grandparents. Whatever the case, these grants remain a stable source of income, although they are often supplemented with other income sources such as part-time jobs and informal businesses.

Third, there is a high dependence on government services. Statistics South Africa reported in 2019 that social grants were the second source of income for most households in the country, following salaries. Evidently, in 2023, almost 50 per cent of the population depended on the Social Security grant. The government compensates the BoP segment by providing social grants and other services, such as housing, health care and sanitation. This makes the South African BoP unique because its purchasing power is also partly influenced by the government. The high number of people who rely on government services often leads to many service delivery protests, as this may seem the only option when services break down. However, no evidence suggests that *izikhothane* have participated in these protests. The topics of income sources and protests in South Africa are complex and beyond the scope of this book; relevant as an explanation of the context in which *izikhothane* live.

Fourth, the unique spatial planning of townships is a creation of the apartheid government. Through its Group Areas Act of 1950, the apartheid government sought to separate black people from white people. Black people were only allowed into urban areas to serve the needs of white people as employees (Ellapen 2007) and were heavily controlled through the implementation of 'pass laws'. Those who did not qualify to work in urban areas had to carry a 'pass' valid for 72 hours, after which they would be arrested (Ellapen 2007: 115). Although these laws were abolished along with the apartheid regime, the legacy of apartheid spatial planning remains. Most black people in townships still travel to urban areas for work, shopping, education and leisure activities (Pernegger & Godegart 2017). The belief that urban areas are superior to townships remains strongly engraved in the minds of *izikhothane*, who prefer to do their shopping in town. This requires *izikhothane* to travel long distances to access these shopping facilities, such as in the Johannesburg Central Business District, even when township malls may sell the same brands.

Finally, although poverty remains deeply entrenched in South Africa, some people have benefited from the transition to a democratic dispensation through various government development policies. This has resulted in the growth of the black middle class and migration into middle-class areas. Black middle-class people who have escaped poverty still have ties with families and siblings in the townships (Southall 2016), which means that BoP consumers 'do not feel as far removed from their aspirational lives' (Lappeman et al. 2019: 327). Such ties between the newly emerged black middle class and the BoP consumers are evident in the lives of *izikhothane*, especially when one considers how some of them depend on relatives with stable employment, such as 'elder brothers', to 'help them out' during tough times (Richards 2015).[5]

Among the characteristics of the BoP population segment that I have discussed, two require more academic attention: brand consciousness and the need for dignity and self-esteem.

Research on the BoP conducted thus far has focused on an analysis of the importance of big national and multinational corporations directing their marketing to the world's poor – who earn about $2 per day – due to the potential profitability of this market (Gupta & Srivastav 2015; Prahalad 2005; Prahalad & Hammond 2002). The rationale is that this market is four billion times larger than the wealthier sectors in the developed world, hence promising growth potential in market share (Prahalad 2005). India is considered to have the largest BoP market in the world, estimated at 925 million people, which is over 23 per cent of the total global BoP market (Gupta & Srivastav 2015). Therefore, it is unsurprising that most studies that have focused on the BoP market have emerged from India or been led by Indian scholars. Catering to this large 'forgotten' segment, as expressed by former President Roosevelt, may seem noble regarding poverty alleviation and improving consumer well-being (Prahalad & Hart 2002; Prahalad 2005), but the fascinating aspect of this market is its hunger for conspicuous consumption, which is described as aspirational consumption (Prahalad & Hammond 2002), consumption that represents aspirations.

The BoP population segment, which is also called the subsistence market in some literature (Viswanathan et al. 2005), tends to subsist under circumstances of deprivation and generally lacks access to basic needs such as education, dignified housing, comfortable and extended transportation facilities, healthy foods and decent education. Further, studies that investigate the consumption behaviour of poor people often define them as those who live below the poverty line yet seem to dedicate most of their earnings to consuming things that neither alleviate their poverty nor satisfy a primary need for consuming a particular good (Moav & Neeman 2008). Literature on consumption patterns of the poor suggests that they have limited income or means to satisfy their needs. Hence, they usually try to do so in the least expensive way possible (Banerjee & Duflo 2007: 147). However, this is not always the case; interestingly, how poor people spend their financial means of survival sometimes counters expectations that would otherwise be dictated by rationality. They may engage in consumption that does not seek to enable them to improve their condition of deprivation (Lamont & Molnar 2001; Moav & Neeman 2008; Posel 2010).

The notion of aspiration features quite prominently in understanding the consumption behaviour of the BoP segment of the population. To aspire is to see and understand where you are vis-à-vis where you want to be. Generally, as Gupta and Srivastav (2015) explain, the ideas that people have about happiness and a meaningful life largely revolve around their aspirations. Thus, when people aspire, they direct their thoughts, feelings and behaviours towards achieving goals that they see as contributing to their well-being. A goal-driven life is essential for people's well-being (Frisch 1998). Goals are not random, as they can be distinguished from each other. Tim Kasser and Richard Ryan (1996) note that there are two categories of goals: intrinsic and extrinsic. They explain that intrinsic goals are linked to personal growth, emotional intimacy, and community service, while extrinsic goals are characterised by attaining financial success, being considered physically attractive (image-centred), and achieving social popularity (fame) (Kasser & Ryan 1996). People engage in these goals to achieve other ends (Kasser & Ryan 1996: 208). In this sense, intrinsic goals are primarily congruent with satisfying basic psychological needs that are inherent to human beings, such as self-acceptance.

By contrast, extrinsic goals have an external orientation, meaning they 'primarily entail obtaining contingent external approval and rewards' (Kasser & Ryan 1996: 280). The external orientation implies that for this goal to be achieved, a third person needs to 'judge' the individual and pronounce the achievement. Without this confirmation, the individual who holds an extrinsic goal will not feel they have achieved it. Brdar et al. (2009) opine that extrinsic goals depend on time and society and tend to be related to objects of fashion, status symbols, and attractiveness. They caution that there must be a balance between intrinsic and extrinsic goals because negativity will likely result from an imbalance where the external orientation overpowers the internal orientation goals. A relentless pursuit of extrinsic goals could harm different aspects of an individual's well-being. This notion of aspiration may also help us get a better understanding of the consumption that characterises BoP consumers.

CONSUMPTION, MASCULINITIES AND *IZIKHOTHANE*

As noted above, people at the BoP are inclined to pursue conspicuous consumption and often do this to satisfy their extrinsic goals (Gupta & Srivastav 2015). A common explanation given by researchers is that BoP consumers try to be or to at least appear to be on the same social level as more affluent members of their society and try to do this through the accumulation of visible material goods that confer social status and compensate for their own perceived dispossession or dissatisfaction (Christen & Morgan 2005; Dreze & Nunes 2009). It is, however, important to note that, as Hill and Gaines (2007) caution, BoP consumers do not necessarily engage in conspicuous consumption to achieve extrinsic goals.

Though the concept of subculture itself has come under academic scrutiny in recent years, it continues to offer insights into understanding *ukukhothana*. The concept of subculture has evolved from perceiving subcultures as deviant and resistant to societal values. The phenomenon of *ukukhothana* presents a form of discursive resistance that seeks to subvert notions of poverty and related identities rather than subverting societal values. This relates to the concept of counter-conduct discussed in the previous chapter; it resists simplistic categorisations. This unique form of resistance makes it difficult to speak of the behaviour of *izikhothane* as a form of conspicuous consumption that follows Veblen's and Simmel's (1957) emulation model. In this sense, the nature of *izikhothane*'s consumption requires more nuanced explanations that consider its context and purpose. This is because consumption is never without a purpose.

Ukukhothana is undoubtedly one of the most peculiar subcultures in post-apartheid South Africa. In *ukukhothana*, the extreme nature of conspicuous consumption is geared towards performing masculine identity. Conspicuous consumption is used in the performance of masculinities in societies that remain patriarchal: where the man's ability to provide tends to entitle him to certain privileges. In this sense, we also begin to see the hegemonic ideals of masculinities being pursued. In this context, then, aspirations are likely to play a very critical role.

Notes

1. The word 'barbarian' originated from the Greek word 'barbarous'. It described people who did not speak Greek, including Persians, Egyptians, Medes and Phoenicians (Pruitt 2016). 'Barbarous' was onomatopoetic; it meant 'blabber'. This is because, to the Greek ear, any foreign language was unintelligible and sounded like 'bar bar bar'. Hence, those people and their cultures became known as barbaric (Seyyedi & Akhlaghi 2013; Smith 2017; Winkler 2017) and the term continued to be applied in various contexts. In a contemporary context, it is a derogatory term to describe a foreign culture or behaviour.

2. Smith MD (2017) Senate passes bill to remove mention of 'barbaric cultural practices' from Harper-era Law. *National Post* 12 December. https://nationalpost.com/news/politics/senate-passes-bill-to-remove-mention-of-barbaric-cultural-practices-from-law-passed-by-harper-conservatives

3. Often, the synonymous phrases 'base of the pyramid' and 'bottom of the pyramid' are used interchangeably in academic literature (Kernani 2007). In this book, however, I use the latter.

4. Mkhize V (2014) 12 Arrested During Violent Thembisa Protest. *Eye Witness News*, 29 August. Accessed 24 July 2019, https://ewn.co.za/2014/08/29/12-people-arrested-in-Thembisa

5. The support the middle class often provides to their relatives who remain stuck in the BoP, colloquially called 'black tax', is defined as the 'burden of having to share your salary with every family member' (see: N Ngwadla. The burden of black tax. *Drum*, 9 March 2018. https://www.fin24.com/Money/the-burden-of-black-tax-20180309). I find it historically interesting that this statement is articulated in an article published in *Drum* magazine, given its target audience as well as its role during the apartheid regime as part of the black press. Though I understand the sentiment and implications of having family dependents – a situation that confronts most black middle-class people in post-apartheid South Africa – one's family is not a burden.

4 Rehumanisation through consumption

In previous chapters, I have discussed how the BoP segment of the population tends to engage in conspicuous consumption to conceal their dehumanising state of impoverishment. Across the globe, at different times and in different ways, sartorial expression, including conspicuous consumption, has been used to challenge unjust racial, social and economic orders (Corrigal 2015; Fleminger 2007; Friedman 1994: 176–177; Magubane 2014; Mentges 2004; Veblen 1899/2003). This chapter discusses the link between consumption and rehumanisation within the subculture of ukukhothana.

Although my research focused on The Good Fellas, I also draw parallels between them and another *izikhothane* crew from Daveyton – the Via Daveytons – that I studied in 2015. In doing this, I draw particularly on Carol Tulloch's (2010: 274) tripartite structure of 'style-fashion-dress' to argue that *izikhothane* are – contrary to the notorious public outrage – involved in articulating a creative set of notions of black male masculinity that work to rehumanise members amid economic, racial and other forms of marginalisation that characterise their post-apartheid lives.

Douglas and Isherwood (1979: 11) point out that consumption is not just a random acquisition of goods and services, but activity patterned in specific ways. The process of consumption takes place with the intention of achieving certain goals that may extend beyond the intrinsic utilitarian value of the consumed commodities or services as a means of communicating identity and cultural values, as well social circumstances (Mnisi 2015: 342). Goods and services that as people consume act as markers of social identity (Lury 1996: 14) and are concerned with meaning, values and communicational aspects (Douglas & Isherwood 1979: 11).

This book is especially interested in Veblen's 1899/2003 concept of conspicuous consumption – 'that which is judged extravagant, luxurious or wasteful' (Campbell 1995: 38). The concept is widely used in contemporary cultures, where consumption is prevalent, and relates to the ways in which people seek to display and make visible to others their wealth, social position and status.

In *The Theory of the Leisure Class*, Veblen (1899) points out that conspicuous consumption is a leading mechanism of social change. Following Simmel's 'trickle down' perspective, Veblen proposes that people's social preferences are established in relation to other people's positions in the social hierarchy (Sassetelli 2007). However, the trickle-down perspective has been largely criticised in recent years, with the leading critique being that it suggests the less fortunate only aspire to emulate those stationed above them and fail to generate their own fashions (Campbell 1987, 1995; Sassetelli 2007; Trigg 2001). It fails to consider, for example, how the poor creatively adapt fashions to meet their aspirations. Also, literature on conspicuous consumption patterns of the poor suggests that poor people often sacrifice scarce resources to acquire expensive goods and services in ways that the trickle-down perspective does not grasp (Banerjee & Duflo 2007; Charles et al. 2009; De Fraja 2009; Griskevicius et al. 2007; Kaus 2010; Mnisi 2015; Moav & Neeman 2010: 413–419).

On the surface, consumption patterns can define and establish a social class, such as the black middle class in South Africa. The idea of a black middle class can be traced before the democratic dispensation in South Africa, for example, the emergence of the black middle class in Mthatha as described by Nkululeko Mabandla (2013). However, it was not until post-1994 that the class witnessed significant growth and recognition (Southall 2016).

It is no surprise that having been previously oppressed and denied humanising opportunities, a segment of black people in South Africa have been identified as being 'middle class', with the freedom and capacity to engage in consumption without exclusion (Iqani 2015; Posel 2010; Southall 2016). This is evidenced in the upsurge of black expenditure after 1994, when more black people had access to money, not only for necessities but also for luxuries, designer brands, property and cars. This was mainly made possible by the new economic policies and social grants (Posel 2010; Southall 2016). In a way, consuming and conspicuously displaying the consumption became symbols of freedom (Corrigall 2015; Iqani 2015; Posel 2010). Conspicuous consumption became a way to assert 'racial pride'; thus, South Africa became a 'nation of shoppers' (Southall 2016). Conspicuous consumption now plays a significant role in the black middle class as a potential signifier of black success and as a rehumanising strategy enacted to offset the consequences of dehumanisation.

There is a need to clarify the concepts of dehumanisation and rehumanisation; as such, we borrow largely from the seminal work of Oelofsen (2009). Although her work is largely a philosophical treatise, she brings these concepts into fresh perspective by applying them to the context of cultural identity and noting their intersectionality with race, class and gender.

The act of dehumanisation takes place during situations of protracted violence (Moller & Deci 2010) in which a society develops a conflictive ethos. At the centre of dehumanisation is the treatment of the enemy 'other' as less than human (Bar-Tal 2000; Oelofsen 2009). In South Africa, the apartheid regime was a situation of protracted violence in which a conflictive ethos resulted in the perceived enemy 'other' – in this case, black people – becoming dehumanised. The colonial history of South Africa, as well as the apartheid regime, were dehumanising faces on the same coin. The socioeconomic, psychological, and political effects were long-lasting and remain evident at various levels.

Dehumanisation occurs through exclusion and maltreatment, which result in perceiving 'the other' as less worthy or 'the self' as more worthy of moral consideration (Oelosfen 2009). The general features of dehumanisation include concentrating on differences and treating the perceived enemy based on the identified differences. This results in denying that the perceived enemy is autonomous and free, or even capable of change (Oelosfsen 2009), thus reducing the other to a stereotype. This one-dimensional view sees the other as an object to which one can ascribe certain absolute features and traits. It is interesting to note that not only the victims of dehumanisation are affected during times of protracted violence, but also those engaged in dehumanising practices; to undermine the humanness of another necessitates the removal of the humanising aspects of the self (Oelofsen 2009). Oelofsen argues that to be human requires an ability to acknowledge and recognise others as human; the failure thereof dehumanises the self as much as the perceived enemy other is dehumanised.

As all parties are dehumanised during situations of protracted violence, the process of dehumanisation requires the rehumanisation of all the 'selves' (victims, perpetrators, bystanders and beneficiaries). As such, the antithesis of dehumanisation, rehumanisation, necessitates reimagining one's prevailing reality with consequences and an interplay between treatment and perception (Oelofsen 2009). Thus, rehumanisation is essentially the act of restoring human dignity. This act is symbolic and translates to behaviours indicative of intrapersonal processes. As a meaning-making process, it is deeply interlinked with one's sense of identity.

Through the concept of 'world' travelling, the idea that to rehumanise, one must imaginatively move from one's own world to the world of the other to understand that the perceived enemy is no different from the self (Lugones 1987). This will result in a change of perception and treatment (Oelofsen 2009). Oelofsen notes there are three steps to engage in during the process of rehumanisation. The first step is to interrogate your own life circumstances and history to understand why you are in a particular situation. The second step is to see yourself as the other sees you. Of course, this is not easy and cannot be objective. If the other's perception of you conflicts with your self-perception, you must investigate why. This will motivate a behaviour change. The final step is to see the other in their own historical and social context, to understand what could possibly lead to the perception and treatment of them.

Dehumanisation through the invention of race

The onset of global economic integration, the dawn of the seaborne empire, the conquest of the Americas, and the rise of the Atlantic slave trade were all key elements in the genealogy of race (Winant 2000).

The concept emerged over time as a kind of world-historical bricolage, an accretive process that was in part theoretical but much more centrally practical. Though intimated worldwide in innumerable ways, racial categorisation was a European invention (Winant 2000) designed to serve European interests.

In this sense, race as a concept was thought of as constituting humans into different biologically distinct sub-species (During 2005). Criteria for these biological definitions often shifted according to pragmatic and legal precedents that necessitated a shift in ideology (Taylor & Spencer 2004; Warnke 2007). Medical evidence was often cited for biological assertions of what became the basis of scientific racism (Cheng 2008). Scientists worked towards substantiating the belief that races are biologically objective categories that exist independently of human classifying activities. For example, at one point difference in blood type was the dominant criterion for differentiating between races (Alland 2002).

The desire to account for what was perceived as abnormal spurned a new discourse about the other. The evidence of abnormality was knowledge acquired through the gaze. The black body came to be considered as a less-than-developed species that lacked the fundamental human ingredients of whiteness. For example, black speech was compared to baby talk and considered underdeveloped (Mnisi & Ngcongo 2023: 345). This and other bodily evidence were cited as proof that the black (other) could not possibly be human. The black person was objectified, thus rendering blackness as ontological – a process of 'thingification' that allowed white power to enact rituals in accordance with the black person's status as a thing. The dehumanised black person could now be owned, bought, sold, beaten or even killed. Ultimately, the work of dehumanisation makes it easy for perpetrators to carry out atrocities (Sereny 1974 in Oelofsen 2009).

Separating the population into different races no doubt served an important function in the history of global social relations. Indeed 'arguments for inherent differences among categories of people are particularly well received in social systems in which access to status, power, and wealth is unequal' (Perry 2007: 15). Race, for example, was an important way of legitimising colonial expansion and the slave trade, which came with great benefits for the initiators of these institutions (during 2005). The races that were thought of as inferior (predominantly classified as black), often suffered from the harsh consequences that resulted from the uneven distribution of resources from slavery and colonialism (West 2001: 1–8).

Within the South African context, the apartheid regime transformed racial relations in a unique way. Although the pre-apartheid South African was governed racially through a loose configuration of laws, the comprehensive apartheid laws (Dubow 2014) created a strict hierarchical ordering of the different races in the country. From the bottom-up, the caste consisted of Africans (blacks), coloureds, Indians and at the top, whites. The legislated racial classification system became the official method to determine race in the country. The recognised tests for determining who was classified, where, consisted of birth records, physical appearance and general community acceptance (Reddy 2000: 130–140). These apartheid racial classification laws were regularly amended to account for seemingly borderline cases. But the laws were designed to systematically silence those at the bottom of this race caste; as a result, dehumanisation became legitimised.

Given this deep legacy of marginalisation that has led to dehumanising conditions, rehumanisation manifests itself in subtle ways in post-conflictive societies such as South Africa. Practices of rehumanisation do not always take on expected or even conventional means. This is the case where sartorial expression through artefacts is concerned. Given the nuanced ways in which the quest for rehumanisation can take in satire of a consumerist sort, it is important to give weight to the argument through compelling exemplars. In the following sections, the chapter examines how *La Sape* of Congo, the diamond dandies, *oswenka* and *izikhothane* illuminate our understanding of rehumanisation through practices of conspicuous consumption. As such, the next section explores the role of sartorial expression/excess in this activity of rehumanisation.

Rehumanisation through sartorial expression: Style-fashion-dress

Sartorial expression is the use of clothes as social skin in the performance of self-expression. As such, the identity one wishes to express depends on one's conception of the self and the social and historical contexts. Material belongings systematically influence how other people's identities are perceived (Dittmar 2008: 27). People use material possessions to express who they are and to construct a sense of who they would like to be. For example, using objects of wealth can fulfil various psychological functions, such as giving people a sense of control, independence, enjoyment or even emotional comfort (Dittmar 2008). This appears to be a motivation of *izikhothane*; through objects, they can fulfil some of their alleged needs.

From Tullock's tripartite structure of style-fashion-dress (2010), a distinction is made between each of these terms. Tullock (2010) brings this idea forth through the questions Which?, When?, How? The idea of style has to do with a unique strategy that a person employs when wearing their clothes in such a way that they 'go well' as an outfit by asking, 'Which one and with what?' The concept of fashion relates to time, the 'When?' in the tripartite structure. Fashion thus relates to the question, 'When is something appropriate?'. As such, it speaks to the relevance of something at a given time. Finally, the question 'How?' asks how the style, in relation to fashion (the time), is presented to achieve the desired outcome of the act of sartorial expression. The sartorial expression project should be considered a deliberate and conscious act with a predefined outcome. From this perspective, failure to correctly apply the tripartite structure would result in a failure to present the intended identity (Tullock 2010). When one signals, observers ought to interpret it the same. As such, the process of making meaning must be consensual amongst members of a particular culture (Douglas & Isherwood 1979). This takes place in the context where how people are treated changes according to the interpretation of their style of dress.

Four examples of groups of dehumanised black African men are the black 'dandy' of the mid-1880s (known as the 'diamond fields dandy'), *oswenka* from South Africa, *La Sape* from Congo, and *izikhothane*.

These three groups found prominence during the colonial and apartheid eras. As noted earlier, the concern here is with, among other things, the circumstances in which these less-than-wealthy men appeared to engage increasingly in conspicuous consumption for purposes that cannot be reduced to emulation or simplistic modes of social reproduction.

'The dandy' was initially a reference to a working-class European male during the Industrial Revolution who used sartorial expression to mimic aristocratic men. This mimicry symbolically suggested that the dandy was a member of the leisure class and claimed the status of a 'pseudo-aristocrat' in the sense of being a 'clothes-wearing man' (Botz-Bornstein 1995; Corrigall 2015). As Corrigall (2015) discusses, dandyism went beyond transgressing class boundaries; it was a political act that questioned the conventions that governed society. The South African 'diamond fields dandy' could be found in the mid-1880s in Kimberly (Magubane 2004). The diamond fields dandies – predominantly black mineworkers – sought to challenge racially inscribed and dehumanising identities and stereotypes (Corrigall 2015; Oelofsen 2009). Through parades of sartorial excess, they rebelled against demands for black people's silence in a white bigot culture and created an identity outside of work (Corrigall 2015).

Years later, a different kind of dandy, *oswenka*, emerged in Johannesburg. *Oswenka* took sartorial excess beyond simply parading to competing against other dandies. The case of *oswenka* represents a group of men who had been stripped of their masculine dignity by the harsh and oppressive conditions to which they were subjected under apartheid. When the subculture first emerged in Jeppestown during the 1950s, *oswenka* were predominantly isiZulu-speaking[1] working-class South African men who migrated to Johannesburg from the rural areas of KwaZulu-Natal and were subjected to the harsh conditions of hostel living during the apartheid era. As defined in the 'Advanced Oxford Dictionary', the name *oswenka* derives from the English word 'swank', which refers to behaving in a way that is self-satisfied, poised and extremely self-confident (Wehmeier et al. 2007: 1492). The men would dress up elegantly in expensive tailored suits and colourful two-toned brogues with well-known European labels and hold amateur fashion shows every few weeks (Fleminger 2007). At these fashion shows, the men competed to out-dress each other. Consumption, here, seems to have provided a means of 'touching base' with aspects of themselves that could otherwise not be publicly displayed; in other words, the exaggerated display of luxury clothing enhanced their sense of self (Kleine et al. 1993). Arguably, through conspicuous consumption, the men in the *oswenka* group sought to reclaim some measure of social status and respect that had been taken away. It would be erroneous to say that they participated in the competitions for the tangible prizes, as these were in no way equivalent to the expenses they incurred to participate in the practice and look the part. For example, the winner might be awarded a cut of the entrance fee, which was not even close to the price of a single suit (Fleminger 2007).[1] Moving away from the South African context, a similar trend of conspicuous consumption emerged in the youth clubs of Bacongo during the 1960s; those who participated in these practices called themselves *La Sape* (Friedman 1994).

La Sape, adapted from the word *saper*, meaning to dress elegantly (Friedman 1994), is a French acronym adopted by the Congolese that stands for *Societe des Ambianceurs et des Personnes Elegantes*'; which in English is 'The Society of Atmosphere Setters and Elegant People' (Friedman 1994: 128; Nedelcu 2009). *La Sape* are predominantly unemployed, unmarried male youths who rank local *couturiers* on a scale that progresses from imported, ready-to-wear clothing at the bottom to *haute couture*, exclusive custom-fitted clothing at the top. They compete individually in their strivings to attain the position of a 'grand', which is a magnificent appearance (Friedman 1994: 128).

The displays of *La Sape*, composed of youths deprived of their political and bureaucratic positions in the Congo, can be traced back to when the first French colonists arrived in the region (Nedelcu 2009). Under the colonisation of Belgium and France, the Congolese people experienced brutality and slavery while the country's natural resources were exploited and depleted (Vanthemsche 2006). However, the Congolese were inspired by the fashion sense the Europeans introduced and perceived French white men as more elegant and literate than they were (Nedelcu 2009). This is a form of dehumanisation called idolisation, in which the dehumaniser is idolised (Oelofsen 2009). Since colonial times in the Congo, clothing has been definitive in social differentiation (Friedman 1994: 122), although the wave of fashionable consumption that was embodied by *La Sape* was more intensive (Friedman 1994).

The final example, *izikhothane,* is substantiated by data from over six months in the field with a select group of ten members of the leading *izikhothane* group from Daveyton, east of Johannesburg at the time, known as the Via Daveytons. This group provided a point of entry into subculture and styles of communication, and following prolonged engagements with the participants, I discovered that the use of sartorial excess to rehumanise the self was indeed part of their rationale. The excerpts below (Mnisi 2015: 349) provide an insightful point of departure for the discussion of *umkhothana* subculture:

> To describe how I feel mangiba khotha [when I 'lick'/ defeat them] there is one word, my man: alive! You see, man, like in our society, especially at school we are made to feel like we are useless, if we are not doing well in our academics and, I mean, to be looked down upon, man, is quite discouraging. But you see, when I do this, man, I know that people feel me and they respect me, because then I know I'm good at something, you know, and it is quite encouraging. (Sifiso, 20 years)

> And what makes me feel important is when people notice me and feel my presence and through my lifestyle, you know, the clothes I wear and the alcohol I drink, really turns a lot of heads. (Kagiso, 19 years)

The two quotes bring several revelations about this sartorial subculture. The youths have been dehumanised through being made to feel less significant; youths whom their society has derided. This is in line with my observation that children tend to inherit and remain in the same social class as their parents, supported by the evidence of enduring entrapment experienced by most 'born frees' whose working-class parents are menial labourers, domestic workers, factory floor workers, and unable to afford leisure lifestyles. The education system still mirrors the hierarchical ordering of apartheid; those from the marginalised races can seldom access education opportunities due to lingering economic inequalities. Ironically, South Africa is touted as 'the rainbow nation' – perhaps the lingering post-apartheid adage holds true here – the rainbow does not include the colour black.

It can be argued that the *izikhothane* use consumption to communicate an identity presumably congruent with their sense of self amid such post-apartheid conditions. From Sifiso's comment that 'at school we are made to feel useless', it is evident that due to their perceived lack of academic inclination, *izikhothane* are perceived as no good and without any prospect of a brighter future. The feeling that you are 'good at something' comes from an interrogation of the self and is based on how you assume others perceive you. Oelofsen (2009) discusses this idea as a step towards rehumanisation. She writes that it is important to search the self to see why others perceive you the way they do, and if what you find is not in line with what others see, then you should act to show that this is not the case. In this sense, Sifiso suggests that – through sartorial excess – he is neither useless nor a failure. He is good at participating in *umkhothana* and this makes him feel encouraged and alive.

The argument can be put forward that most *izikhothane* emanate from circumstances that make them feel less significant; even less than human. In most cases, they highlight protracted poverty as a dehumanising factor in their lives; thus they try to dissociate themselves from the identity of poverty. This is apparent in the quote below (Mnisi 2015: 80):

> Eeeeh my brother uyadlala wena [you are playing] you see when we gather for a session we make sure that we have food like boma [such as] pizza, KFC, Ultra Mel you know and consume it there in front of people. We don't eat the food in order to fill up our stomach ... no man it is so that people can see what we can afford. (Kagiso)

Something else to consider here is that paternalism – when a person is perceived as incapable of making wise decisions or having a sense of agency – is one form of dehumanisation (Oelofsen 2009). *Izikhothane*, similar to *oswenka* and *La Sape*, found themselves stripped of their dignity and made to feel less significant. Through conspicuous consumption, their significance becomes evident because material goods have identity-creating and -enhancing features (Dittmar 2008: 35). Through this kind of consumption, they can create their own desired identity in society, thus demonstrating a sense of agency that refuses to be identified with a failed class of society (Mnisi 2015).

Through conspicuous consumption, *izikhothane* seek to humanise themselves and reclaim their sense of self. As with *La Sape*, who were not considered rich due to their sartorial parades and the diamond fields dandies, who were not respected or valued, *izikhothane*'s marginalised conditions still prevailed and remained unchanged; only the way they perceived themselves changed.

What, then, do we make of this? I argue that *izikhothane*'s activities represent their aspirations to be 'human' and, as such, are possibly the pursuit of aspirational rehumanisation. Their activities represent 'self-rehumanisation' and not 'other rehumanisation'. A second layer of this aspiration is that of masculine identity. Indeed, the exemplars in this book indicate that masculinity is a key trait that the subcultures mentioned have in common.

Rehu(man)ised: Consumption and masculinities

Within a patriarchal society, a society that is built on the foundation of male supremacy, gender is assumed to be the primary determinant of social influence. Men are given the position of power, thus discriminating against women, although there are studies in literature that suggest the opposite, that a patriarchal system oppresses men as much as it may seem to function in their favour (Wilson 2000). The attributes that make a male figure 'a man' in such societies include physical power, economic stability (which may be achieved by owning a business or having a job and being able to provide for one's family), heterosexuality and being emotionally strong. Further, all these features, excluding physical power, still form the foundation of manhood in the township of Daveyton where the *Via Daveytons* are based. While participants in the study aspire to be 'real men', they never mention physical power as an essential trait that makes up this figure. From interviews conducted with the members of the *Via Daveytons* (Mnisi 2015) and also later with The Good Fellas, it was apparent that being a masculine man is essential to being a proper subject of respect in society. Below are some of the responses from the participants:

> ... you have to be a man who is employed and wear expensive clothes such as Roberto Botticelli, like Italian clothes and with nice cars. People need to look at you and be able to say we have never seen this guy struggling. (Sifiso)

> ... a man is a man by his home ... Hahaha this just reminds of a joke that we used to use to *diss* [disrespect] people. We used say a man is defined by his shoe. So if you didn't have this shoe you would be called a boy. The shoes that made a man were the Rossimoda and Arbiter. We would just start stomping our shoes, and if you would come wearing your new Nike snickers you would be ostracised. But basically what makes a man in our community is your dignity as a person, and obviously you will need money because you can't do anything without money. (Skhumbuzo)

> To be honest without money, man, if you just look down and out, no one is going to respect you as a man. So you need to appear as this person who has money, then you will be respected. (Kagiso)

> As a man you have to prove to people that you have money, but in a good way, not in a bad way, like laughing at the misery of others. Women will like you and you know, man, *izikhothane* love women, and that makes you a man, you know. Also making good decisions that are beneficial to you and your family. Obviously as we grow older this thing of being a *s'khothane* will end but for now our age allows us and it is part of growing up. Rather grow up through having fun, dressing well, having women and being happy than being a drug addict! (Rabbi)

I only ran my cigarette-selling business at school and did not want people *ekasi* (township) to know that I had such a business because I had a lifestyle that I had to present. All I wanted people to see was a man who has money and could spend [it] in any way he wanted, not how he generated it. (Man-E)

… and obviously, as a man, you need three things: clothes, alcohol, and girls! If you have this combination you are sorted. And I must say that, man, being a *s'khothane* has really groomed me. I have a lot of experience, man. I know more than what other guys my age know about sex. I enjoy my life, man. Also, protection is very important: when having sex, [it] is important because if not, man, you'll end up looking like a skeleton. (Mthingo)

You see, going forward as a man I want to be a confident man, one who is responsible and is capable of getting things done. I want to be the kind of man whom a woman can look at and be sure that I can provide for her and go far with her in life. I do not want to be a lazy man waking up at 10 am in the morning. I mean by that time real men have already made thousands, and this would just show how unreliable you are and how impossible it would be for you to build a home. (Vega)

For now, I am still young and as a man, you know, girls form an important part of your life. I have nine girlfriends now and I manage them quite well. Even though sometimes electric wires get into contact with each other and minor explosion results. I still try and control them and ensure that my girls never meet. Unfortunately, I am still too young to commit to one girl, man, so I push as many as I can. Until I find the one, this is how it will be. I am not a bad person. I am just young. (Katlego aka Skopo)

Notably, similar comments on what makes a man in this community appear in all the quotes above – evident financial stability.

Economic stability results from having money; without money, one would not be respected as a man. Skhumbuzo states that 'you can't do anything without money'. The marker of manhood is, thus, one's ability to consume, which is made possible by having access to money. This does not come as a surprise, given the socioeconomic status of most black South African men who continue to experience the dehumanising legacy of the apartheid regime.

In the quotes above, the sartorial excess becomes a method that enables people to regain a sense of self, dignity and respect. These are the elements involved in any project of rehumanisation. In the three steps of rehumanisation through 'world' travelling (Lugones 1987) it becomes apparent that a certain level of self-actualisation and rehumanisation is achieved. This happens through imagination and symbolically inserting the self into the leisure class through sartorial expression. There are limitations to this imagination and 'world' travelling. The main limitation rests on the premise that reality sometimes presents harsh reminders that one has not yet actually arrived at the point of the ideal self.

Although this kind of consumption does not necessarily seem to liberate those who engage in it from the oppression they face, what it does manage to achieve is a change in the perception of the self and the perceived ability to reclaim the loss of respect and dignity from one's reference group. In other words, it is difficult to say with certainty whether rehumanisation occurs, but the perception of rehumanisation by those engaged in it seems to be a sufficient starting point. This is evident since the signalling was mainly done in the presence of the oppressed reference groups, not necessarily in the spaces that the oppressors occupied. This idea is indicative of aspirational consumption (Mnisi 2015), which I explore in chapter six. As Magubane (2004) discusses, sartorial excess becomes a mechanism that enables black people to reclaim their body from white domination. Thus, the apparent aggressive pursuit of leisure works to establish the autonomous nature of black pleasure. When dress and fashion are considered as 'social skins', they allow the wearer to reclaim and redefine new social territory (Gondola 2004 in Corrigall 2015).

In his 2005 book *The System of Objects*, French sociologist Jean Baudrillard argues that when a person becomes a consumer, they essentially get into a relationship with the social systems that give their possessions value. The consumption may be of food, clothes, drinks and property. Given that consumption does not take place in a vacuum, it is intercepted by various factors such as social inequality, poverty and social class, which, in the case of South Africa, is also based on race and gender. In economically deprived societies, consuming expensive commodities such as designer-label clothes signals access to resources (Mohamed 2011). This perceived access to resources accorded by the ownership of expensive clothes has its roots in the dehumanising apartheid era, which conflated race, gender and class and curtailed economic possibilities and upward social mobility for black people. Ratele (2012) argues that such structural violence led to the fetishisation of certain clothing brands for some young black men in townships. Somehow, the history of the dehumanising oppression in South Africa, which led to deprivation and exclusion from consumption, has led – as former president Thabo Mbeki noted – to freedom being 'defined not by the ethereal and therefore intangible gift of liberty, but by the designer labels on the clothes we wear' (Posel 2010: 159). This history of oppression and exclusion explains why, in most instances, consumption symbolises freedom.

Notes

1   IsiZulu is one of the 11 official languages of South Africa.
2   See also: Felperin L (2005) Review: The swenkas. *Variety*, 11 Jan. Accessed 12 September 2017 http://www.variety.com/review/VE1117925881?refcatid=31

5 Booty on fire: Looking at izikhothane *through Veblen's lens*

Thorstein Veblen's (2003/1899) critique of the nineteenth-century American leisure class makes it apparent that although their costly, wasteful and showy expenditure was somewhat distasteful, it was in keeping with class expectations of normal behaviour. While he did not focus on the lower classes, he asserted that they did not stand outside the matrix of 'honour' mediated by conspicuous consumption (Veblen 2003). Although their more meagre incomes constrained their consumption, they emulated the higher classes as they, too, vied for status (Veblen 2003: 58). The poor were marginal to Veblen's original thesis, as was a form of consumption that was virtually unknown in Veblen's time, namely the spectacular destruction of expensive commodities by poor people in front of an assembled audience. The destructive conspicuous consumption of *izikhothane* – who consume well beyond what they can comfortably afford – is a possibility that Veblen did not explore.

Ukukhothana in context

At *ukukhothana* performances, participants occasionally tear or burn bank notes as well as their own and their rivals' clothes. They also wash their hands with luxury alcohol and douse expensive food with it after throwing the food on the ground. Common types and brands of alcohol include whiskey like Jameson, cognacs like Bisquit and Hennessy, and imported beers and ciders. As these young men often like to say: 'We drink beer that is only in green bottles, not the brown bottles', an oblique reference to the fact that most beers in brown bottles are produced locally and retail for less than the imported green bottle beers. Unlike most working-class township people who drink Castle Lager, Hansa Pilsner, and Carling Black Label, *izikhothane* buy Heineken, Amstel and Windhoek beers. They also buy popular fast food from franchises that recently infiltrated the township market and are normally associated with affluent people in the township, such as Kentucky Fried Chicken (KFC), Debonairs Pizza and Panarottis.

It is important for these young men to attract a female audience, and rival groups compete to impress the most attractive spectators. Emboldened *s'khothane* often try to court those girls who catch their eye during the performance. The girls on the sidelines of the performance are often perceived as coveted ornaments that add to the performer's credibility as a man worthy of the 'salute'. As the young men often remark of their comrades in isiZulu, '*lo mjita u blind and unstwembu*', township colloquial talk used to praise a person who is good at something and to indicate that they are worthy of respect, the same kind of respect they crave from the audience.

Izikhothane performances happen against a backdrop of poverty. Their expensive outfits often cost more than some of their working-class parents' monthly incomes. Most *izikhothane* come from homes with single parents working as domestic cleaners, factory workers or retail assistants. They often live in shacks, Reconstruction Development Programme (RDP) houses, or rented backyard rooms. While some *izikhothane* live with both parents, others are from child-headed families or have precarious living arrangements with relatives. Against this backdrop, people commonly question how *izikhothane* fund their lifestyle. Notably, in some instances, they receive money from their parents, uncles and other relatives who may or may not know about their engagement in *ukukhothana*. In other instances, they earn money through small informal businesses, such as car washing and selling snacks and drinks. While there are rumours that *izikhothane* steal from individuals and businesses, I am not aware of any case where the *izikhothane* I followed engaged in criminal activities to fund their participation in *ukukhothana*. Instead, they often insisted, '*Itariyane kwamele lispine*' (which translates as 'an Italian must work hard', that is, you must be willing to work hard to become reputable). The money-making and saving were, however, not 'victimless'. Several *izikhothane* reported that they concealed money at home and did not contribute to the household expenses as much as they should have, to save for participating in the performances.

Given their low socioeconomic status, it is important to consider *izikhothane*'s saving and sacrificing activities. Crew members tended to save money for a long time before a performance. Interestingly, few of them owned bank accounts and most saved their cash at home, stashing it secretly, normally in a jar. As many of them assured me, this proximity to their savings offered many temptations and required much discipline to persist. Some young men also saved by buying their clothes on lay-by, a practice whereby local businesses allow customers to pay off an item over a set period and only 'release' the item once it has been fully paid off. The risk with lay-bys is that the purchaser needs to pay them off within three months or lose both the money and the coveted item of clothing.

It is also important to note that not all *izikhothane* events were accompanied by destruction. The crews were strategic about the timing of 'burn events' as it took time to accumulate sufficiently large amounts of valuables to make for a spectacle. Burning only a few items or items with relatively low value could diminish an event's success and damage the crew's reputation. Once they had accumulated the appropriate outfits and created enough anticipation in their followers, they organised events in widely marketed public spaces.

For the most part, *izikhothane* crews preferred to host their main events at places like Witbank Dam near the East Rand, Dries Niemandt Park near Thembisa, Fountains Valley in Pretoria and other public parks. Recently, they also started hosting events at local community halls. Increasingly, these events are incorporated into the entertainment section of other community or public events. For instance, in 2016, The Good Fellas performed at the Miss Masakhane Beauty Pageant, and in 2017 at the Miss Thembisa Beauty Pageant. Apart from these local events, *izikhothane* have featured in commercials and as part of large music festivals. *Izikhothane* choose dates that allow their fellow schoolmates and peers to attend in large numbers. While some crew members might be older, this is largely a subculture for school-going peers.

More mundanely, *izikhothane* have spontaneous gatherings on Friday afternoons just after school. They form large circles on popular road intersections and start dancing and insulting other crew members ('trash talking'). As these gatherings attract more people, taxis with loud sound systems stop to play music for the dancers. The crowds soon disrupt the traffic flow, with many impatient and annoyed motorists trying to inch through the crowds, which eventually part reluctantly. When a competitor runs out of words to 'trash' his opponent, when his clothes are deemed inferior, when he no longer has alcohol to spill, when he refuses to burn or tear his clothes, and when female audiences show enthusiasm and excitement for the other participant, he knows he has been defeated. The prize for a victory is the short-lived honour of having outdone an opponent, at least until the next meeting.

Conspicuous consumption

Veblen wrote *The Theory of the Leisure Class* (1899/2003) at a time of mass industrialisation and social inequality in America. Focusing largely on the leisure class, he asserted that their consumption of goods was seldom if ever, motivated by utilitarian concerns. Rather, men consumed expensive goods and participated in visible leisure habits to signal their wealth in a competition for honour and social distinction. In this system, the possession of property functioned as a basis of popular esteem, which then became a requisite of self-respect or honour.

According to Veblen (1899/2003: 131), '[i]n order to gain and to hold the esteem of men, it is not sufficient merely to possess wealth or power. The wealth or power must be put in evidence, for esteem is awarded only on evidence'. Veblen (2003) found much of this evidence in the lavish parties of the leisure class, which allowed friends and competitors to witness the host's wealth, underscoring his pecuniary strength. Further, Veblen (1899/2003: 75) likened these costly entertainments to potlatches, an economic system of competitive hosting and gift-giving among the indigenous people of the Pacific Northwest Coast of Canada and the United States, as famously described by Franz Boas (1888; see also Benedict 1934; Harris 1974). During a potlatch, the hosting chief and his people demonstrated his wealth (and honour) by showering guests with gifts, providing lavish entertainment and burning expensive consumer items.

Anthropologists have also recorded cases where hosting chiefs burnt their own homes during the potlatch (Benedict 1934; Harris 1974). Guests at these potlatches had to reciprocate in a similar manner at a future date, lest they lose honour.

According to Veblen, such 'waste' was central to how the leisure class demonstrated wealth. Their choice of food, costly clothes, property, banquets, alcohol and cigars went far beyond utility – the 'waste' was primarily honorific (Veblen 1899/2003: 108). Like the potlatch and the lavish entertainments of the nineteenth-century American leisure class, *ukukhothana* is a spectacle of wasteful consumption geared at impressing audiences. However, unlike those spectacles of yore, it is funded by young men who are relatively marginal in terms of social status and wealth.

Veblen's model did not address the possibility of poor people destroying or 'wasting' luxury goods to gain honour. However, he stated that while the competition for distinction through conspicuous consumption was particularly acute among the leisure class, it permeated all levels of society. Men from various levels of life commonly emulated consumption styles and patterns that would distinguish them from people of the same social class. In analysing the lower classes, Veblen (1899/2003: 78) pointed out that ambitious men would emulate those of a higher social class by wearing cheaper versions of elegant clothes. While these copies did not evince the workmanship of the originals, they were distinctly unsuitable for manual labour, an important quality to gain pecuniary honour.

In discussing the consumption patterns of ambitious lower class men, Veblen allowed for emulation but not for the possibility that these men would consume the same expensive items as the leisure class, or that these expenses would exhaust all their wealth. Indeed, he makes the point that for those poor people in nineteenth-century America 'for whom acquisition and emulation is possible' it was only so 'within the field of productive efficiency and thrift' and that 'the struggle for pecuniary reputability will in some measure work out in an increase of diligence and parsimony' (Veblen 1899/2003: 18). However, he later suggests that conspicuous consumption claimed a significant portion of urban dwellers' income because the desire to impress transient observers in these areas was much stronger than it was in rural areas (Veblen 1899/2003: 87).

Despite these qualifications, Veblen' emulation model has been criticised for its reductionism and for overlooking the complex ways people imitate and adapt various consumer goods within different cultural contexts (Sassatelli 2007). Critics have also pointed out that his model does not allow for the poor to invent their own fashions (Sasselli 2007: 68). Contemporary understandings of consumption hold that identification and imitation take place alongside more creative and selective procedures of reproduction (Sasselli 2007: 69; see also Bourdieu 1984).

In *The Theory of the Leisure Class,* Veblen (1899/2003: 18) scathed the frivolous and wasteful expenditure of the rich, but praised the parsimony of the lower classes. Similarly, most people in Johannesburg's townships do not participate in *ukukhothana* and are, like Veblen, disdainful of this 'wasteful' and 'unnecessary' practice. The difference between Veblen's disdain and that expressed in the townships is that disapproval of *ukukhothana* centres on *izikhothane* being 'matter out of place'; as poor young men, they behave unlike others of a similar class who carefully husband their money, or if indebted, do not flaunt their consumption.

Indeed, *izikhothane's* consumption tended to demonstrate identities removed from their 'real' economic circumstances. Considering that most of their parents are working class, the expectation was that they would behave like their parents by buying modest clothes and constraining their expenditures to fit within their meagre means (Burger et al. 2015; Melber 2017). Participants also tended to expect their parents to always disapprove of the 'waste' involved in their performances. Ironically, some parents financially assisted their sons in this lifestyle as an expression of love, although they were not supportive of the destructive aspect of the subculture (Hamilton & Catterall 2006).

Such expressions of filial affection are not explored in the media's treatment of *ukukhothana*. Often the subject of investigative journalism programmes, *izikhothane* have frequently been depicted as irrational, selfish and driven by the obsession to have their proverbial 15 minutes of fame, at whatever cost. In the hard-hitting *3rd Degree* television programme, Debora Patta focused on *ukukhothana* and commented that it was 'bling gone obscenely mad' (Mnisi 2015: 340). Patta's comments on the subculture were in keeping with a wider trend in the media to focus only on the negative aspects of *ukukhothana*. Apart from investigative programming, *izikhothane* have also featured as uncouth braggarts in television advertisements and local soap operas. The most common media narrative is that this is a superficial youth culture in which naïve young men destroy expensive consumer items to attract fleeting attention (TVSA 2012). Many of these narratives are manufactured to create outrage at the supposed moral corruption that sees impressionable young men destroy what their needy audiences could productively have consumed. Not surprisingly, media footage of *izikhothane* is always sensationally filmed against footage of the grinding poverty of the people and settings where they perform.

Izikhothane *in Thembisa*

Lury (1996) suggests that consumption patterns should be read as communication messages with consequence and social meaning (see also Douglas & Isherwood 1979: 11; McCracken 1990). So how did The Good Fellas perceive *ukukhothana* and what were they communicating?

The Good Fellas referred to their expensive purchases in the same way as warriors or plunderers would refer to booty; these items were symbolic of their 'victory' and bestowed honour and respect because they evidenced successful contestation through aggression. Their 'white man's liquor' (Edwards 1988),[1] expensive clothes, girls and choice food all represented booty. In an interview, a member of The Good Fellas noted:

> Being a s'khothane is a competition – you see, we have to let our clothes do the talking. They must tell people that we have money so they can respect us. We know that in reality

we don't have money, boss, we are just guys who hustle in order to be respected as real men ... but during our performance we are wealthy, full stop!

In this 'competition', the achievement of having clothes that 'spoke' for their owner was hard won. Indeed, for many *izikhothane*, their clothes represented an achievement, particularly when one considers the sacrifice that went into acquiring them. According to Veli, an outspoken member of The Good Fellas, 'we know what is trending and then '*Itariyane kwamele lispine*' [an Italian must work hard] in order to have enough money for the clothes.' Hard work and an ability to hustle, however, was often not enough. Many *izikhothane* had to make persistent sacrifices in daily life and forego basics that their peers took for granted. Mpho (Sekatana), for instance, explained that his sacrifice involved not eating during break time at school so that he could save his lunch money for clothes. 'And on top of that, I also sell the Strikers biscuits in order to supplement my saved lunch money,' he said.

Merely having expensive clothes was not enough. As The Good Fellas stated, anyone could acquire expensive clothes through sacrifice. It took courage to publicly burn those same clothes. As Man-E noted, 'We try not to burn or tear clothes, man, because they are very expensive, but when it gets really tough, you would strategically destroy something because that would be the final step in getting people to notice you and see that you are *there*'. This is why it was so important for crews to impress with their dance routines and hone their trashing skills. The better these skills were, and the more the audience was impressed with their presence – with the *izikhothane* being *there* – the less chance they would have to burn their expensive clothes. But this was a careful balancing act; if the boasts were too fulsome they invited 'testing'. In public contests, the only real way to test their rivals' boasts was to tear or burn their clothes. Indeed, this often happened when a rival competitor carried his extra clothes in a backpack, a powerful symbolic signal of excess. In these cases, the backpack was often seized and burnt. To win esteem, the 'victim' had to keep calm when this happened because if he quarrelled about his possessions, he would immediately lose the contest and face humiliation in front of his peers. Vega, a proud Good Fella, expanded on this when he said:

During the mock battle, man, you must be ready for anything. For example, a guy can just be dancing then come to you and tear your T-shirt from the neck down, and you can't fight him because doing that means you can't really afford to be a s'khothane – you are simply claiming *nje* [just]; you are not a real man.

The same manly wastefulness marked The Good Fellas' consumption of alcohol. They did not just drink expensive spirits but incorporated this liquor into their performances, spraying it on their clothes and washing their hands with it. According to one crew member, they did this to say: 'I have more and can afford to waste'.

Beyond its honorific utility, alcohol played an important social role in *ukukhothana*. The Good Fellas enjoyed alcohol as something that 'men do'. Interestingly, with regards to consuming expensive spirits, Maxwell stated that these 'are the bottles, the real alcohol that real men who are wealthy and worthy of respect drink'. Extending the prestige of expensive whiskeys, Snamzo mentioned that 'You could not expect people to respect you if you, like other commoners, drank alcohol like *is'kali* or *intankunyisa;* home brewed alcohol normally sold to old people in *shebeens*'. Essentially, The Good Fellas' consumption of expensive alcohol was economically aspirational; a stylised act that involved the impersonation of an ideal masculinity associated with wealth and success.

Alcohol also played an important role in creating bonds between friends in the group (Dittmar 2008; Friedman 1994). The Good Fellas associated drinking with being happy, with coming together and being free to do as they please without fearing anything. Members of The Good Fellas frequently stated that alcohol allowed them to socialise freely and to prove their loyalty and friendship by taking care of friends who were drunk. Their shared intoxication and hangovers also allowed for the sharing of stories about the previous night's drinking.

Apart from large quantities of alcohol, The Good Fellas also liked smoking a hookah pipe. They insisted that it made them 'cool'. Ever aware of fashions in the city's trendy nightclubs, they pointed out that all the fancy lounge bars had hookah pipes. The hookah gave them a 'head rush' at a much cheaper price than alcohol and, in lean times, hid their lack of cash. Girls perceived them as sophisticated and worldly for smoking the hookah rather than cheap roll-ups (hand-rolled cigarettes) or 'loose draws' (single cigarettes bought at local spaza shops).

Honorific failure?

While The Good Fellas insisted that *ukukhothana* performances, and especially the spectacular burning events, gained them 'respect' as rich men or men of a higher status, they were aware that many outsiders saw them as 'wasteful boys who buy things that they cannot afford'. In this respect, their performances, unlike those of the leisure class, could be said to fail to convey the intended message. Mthingo complained about this:

> Yoh! The problem is that people have an uninformed perception about *izikhothane*, especially when they see us do what we do. They say we are claiming and [that we are] fake people and *siya fosta* [literally, 'we are forcing a version of ourselves that we are not'], [they] even suggest that we should rather do useful things with the money we waste. But there is more to us, man – we are not bad guys! I mean, as the name of our group implies, we are The Good Fellas!

Mpho (Sekatana) added: 'Among *izikhothane* you will surely be saluted but people who are not *izikhothane* will only comment that these kids are burning clothes and this and that. If you really want to be famous among *izikhothane*, you must burn clothes and then you will be a legend'.

The Good Fellas did not seem deterred by negative perceptions of their behaviour. As Maxwell said: 'I don't care about people who criticise me because I know what I'm doing and where I'm going'. Like his fellow Good Fellas, being a *s'khothane* was a fleeting phase of his youth, a period of enjoyment before fulfilling his life goals. These goals were similar to those of his peers at school: to secure a well-paying job, buy a house in a more upmarket area, marry, have children and have a good quality of life. As Snamzo summed up these aspirations:

> I'm currently in Grade 11. Next year I'll be finishing school and after that university follows immediately. I want to go to UJ [University of Johannesburg]. I'm not sure about what I want to study but one thing for sure I want to get a good office job and wear a tie to work.

These were goals for a distant future, and being *izikhothane* was imagined as a carefree hiatus between childhood and responsible adulthood.

Of particular importance to The Good Fellas was that their competitions put them in a position where their impoverished backgrounds were concealed. Most young men in the group remarked that the visibility of poverty, exposed, was painful. Again, the ability to hide their real circumstances was tied to ideas of masculinity untouched by poverty. As Veli remarked: 'Your challenges as a man should not be laid bare for all to see. You need to push your stuff'. But this was not always possible because most *izikhothane* did not have enough expensive clothes to 'push' and had to resort to wearing less expensive items on non-performance days. On an ordinary day, The Good Fellas would hang out at the local taxi rank, chatting with one another wearing old clothes, patched T-shirts, and caps – except for the occasional branded item that punctuated their outfits. In this guise, it was evident that they came from underprivileged backgrounds. It was in these ordinary contexts - when *izikhothane's* brash assertions were threadbare – that older people felt empathy for them.

Veblen (2003) thought the 'leisure class' was particularly guilty of wasteful conspicuous consumption because they put their 'wealth in evidence' through spectacular parties and expensive clothes, in pursuit of honour. While showing off to their peers, the leisure class's excessive consumption also underlined clear class differences, distancing them from the working classes' productive labour and parsimony. People lower down the socioeconomic scale emulated leisure-class styles, but Veblen noted that their consumption was largely derivative and constrained by their limited means.

Neither Veblen nor social commentators in South Africa could have foreseen the rise of *ukukhothana*. Although the diamond field dandies and *oswenka* offer historical examples of poor black men who spent inordinate amounts of money on clothes (and in the latter case, competed for sartorial honours), commentators have been puzzled by *ukukhothana*'s destructive wastefulness, for seemingly dysfunctional and vain ends. From Veblen's perspective, one could also see their performances as failed attempts to gain honour, especially since the young men fooled no one into thinking that they were, contrary to general knowledge, rich or part of the leisure class.

In this chapter, I have tried to dispel some of the perceptions that frame *ukukhothana* in a solely negative light by looking at the ways in which *izikhothane* viewed their competitions and gave meaning to their conspicuous consumption. I have argued that while *izikhothane* wanted to escape their poverty, they did not see the *ukukhothana* lifestyle as a (deluded) way out of poverty. Instead, while wildly aspirant, most *izikhothane* saw their participation in this youth culture as a fun part of their youth and to generate social status among their peers.

Behind the scenes, crews such as The Good Fellas worked hard to buy their expensive clothes and made a lot of sacrifices to allow them to participate in this lifestyle. The rewards included popularity and respect (honour) for being stylish 'hustlers', especially when their hard-earned booty caught fire. Unlike Veblen's lower-class imitators, these young men were deeply creative in the ways that they assembled outfits and mixed branded clothes with cheaper ones. Unlike Veblen's individualists, *izikhothane* were young men who used their conspicuous consumption to create a group identity and cohesion. Thus, there is much more to the *izikhothane's* performances than simply a misplaced hankering after 'honour' or fame.

Note

1   See also Blignaut C & Sithole S (2014) The twisted tale of alcohol and apartheid. News24. Accessed 22 April 2016, http://www.news24.com/Archives/City-Press/Twisted-tale-of-alcohol-andapartheid-20150429

6 Burning to consume? Conspicuous consumption versus aspirational consumption

In 2012 when Debora Patta commented on *ukukhothana* as 'bling gone obscenely mad' (Mnisi 2015: 340), it was a key moment of reflection on the consumption patterns of South Africa's economically marginalised people. Her statement draws attention to the parallel consumption patterns of the poor and the wealthy, with different reception of each pattern by the reference groups.

The emergence of Veblen's nineteenth-century leisure class was met with honour and general awe. It was respected and had a high social status. As Veblen observed, their consumption put their wealth in evidence, hence the concept of conspicuous consumption. Conversely, when *izikhothane* emerged in South Africa, also engaging in what could be akin to conspicuous consumption, they were neither perceived as wealthy nor did they manage to attract respect from society. Instead, their consumption had the opposite effect. They revolted the public and were accused by mainstream media of being 'mad', 'wasteful', and 'blatantly foolish'.[1] Perceptions of their behaviour lacked the honour bestowed upon the leisure class.

This observation raises concerns regarding the acceptance of *izikhothane*'s conspicuous consumption behaviour. This is something else, but what is it? In this chapter, I grapple with the concept of aspirational consumption to possibly explain *ukukhothana*.

On the reliability of the signal: The democratisation of luxury and the erosion of the leisure class

In *The Sum of Small Things: A Theory of the Aspirational Class*, Elizabeth Currid-Halkett, professor of public policy at the University of Southern California, writes (2017: 1): 'Status has always consumed us'. Currid-Halkett's central argument is that consumption choices speak volumes about our social status and economic class positioning. Our prosaic consumption choices provide us with a locus of definitions about who we are and the social groups to which we are members and outsiders. The depth of our consumption behaviour signals positions and dispositions about the social, cultural, economic and even political aspects of our lives that are not easily visible. A fascinating observation about consumption, and in particular conspicuous consumption, is that it has become commonplace with the poor being said to fully participate in it more than the rich. The pervasiveness of conspicuous consumption, which is not curtailed by social positions and economic status, is a result of the democratisation of luxury (Boorstin in Currid-Halkett 2017: 6).

The democratisation of conspicuous consumption, 'The noughties' in 2000–2009, saw a decade of conspicuous consumption. This era was characterised by acquiring expensive designer handbags such as Prada, Armani, Ralph Lauren and Oscar de la Renta. In the communication technologies, Steve Jobs' Apple products, such as the iPhone, iPad, iPod and iMac, communicated affluence. Locally, people bought expensive furniture and large flat-screen televisions, demonstrating a hunger for brands that acted as markers of social status. Some of these products indeed compromised practicality.

However, due to the cost of these commodities, the masses could not afford them; one effect was the growth in demand for counterfeit products, though this interestingly further elevated the status of original brands, argues Barnett (2005). In response to this need, several fashion houses introduced what became known as 'diffusion lines', which are secondary product lines of merchandise introduced by high-end fashion houses sold at a cheaper and more affordable price. An example is Ralph Lauren's Polo, which many South Africans continue to adore.

The advent of mass production democratised luxury by making luxury goods accessible to many people. The Industrial Revolution of the eighteenth century, the context in which Veblen (1899/2003) wrote his treatise, created many newly rich Americans who engaged in conspicuous consumption while the poor emulated them through cheaper versions. The Industrial Revolution is characteristic of modern-day capitalism, which inadvertently opened the floodgates of conspicuous consumption even for the common man (Currid-Halkett 2017: 8). Products that at one point were reserved for the rich became accessible to the newly created middle class. Mass production made it possible to service the growing middle class with authentic consumer items (Currid-Halkett 2017).

In this era, more people earned money by working in the factories, and credit became extended and more accessible. The leisure class of the late nineteenth century owned property and consumed lavishly; however, the twentieth-century middle class also had access to these differentiation features of the leisure class. Most clothing companies and brands decided to cater to the growing middle class by introducing cheaper but authentic diffusion lines. According to Currid-Halkett, this access to conspicuous consumption and other defining characteristics of the leisure class meant that conspicuous consumption had become commonplace. It was no longer possible to distinguish the rich from the poor, and the leisure class was eroded and ended. This effectively throws the emulation model into an imbalance since the central feature of this remains to be counterfeit products.

The South African situation regarding the rise of the middle class – particularly the black middle class – is also interesting. The advent of democracy opened many business and employment opportunities for black people and provided access to credit. This resulted in the growth of the middle class, which engages in conspicuous consumption. However, the ubiquity of conspicuous consumption saw most poor people engaging in it to the detriment of their livelihoods. The emergence of *ukukhothana* speaks to this. Currid-Halkett argues that the leisure class has ceased to exist – not necessarily because it has lost its wealth but due to the change in how one falls into this class. More people have access to the leisure class through hard work as opposed to birthright and, in symbolic terms, through conspicuous consumption in instances where there is no wealth per se.

In this sense, a high social status is no longer attained solely through conspicuous consumption, as anyone can now participate. This has precipitated the emergence of a new class, the aspirational class. Mobility into the upper class or the high echelons of the new order of things is not a birthright or property held for generations; it is through acquiring knowledge. According to Currid-Halkett (2017: 17), 'these new elites are not simply members of an economic group tied to one another by their financial success'. This observation leads to questioning the validity of conspicuous consumption in enabling people to attain a high social status: consider how the conspicuous consumption of *izikhothane* generally engrosses some people while others frown upon it.

Other ways that enable people to elevate their social status are emerging in the townships. One of these is indeed the acquisition of knowledge. This is evident in the entrance of private education in most townships, most of which are owned by companies such as Curro and ADvTECH. Many young parents ensure their children are admitted into these private schools.

Currid-Halkett effectively traces the trajectories of the leisure class and the symbolism of the emergent aspirational class and its erosive consequences in a developed economy. The concept of conspicuous consumption is rooted in the same context. Introducing the concept of the aspirational class to the South African context muddies the waters for three main reasons. Firstly, South Africa is an emerging market with an insignificant upper class. Secondly, the growth of the middle class was and continues to be accelerated by post-apartheid economic reforms. Thirdly, there is a significant consumer segment at the bottom of the pyramid (BoP). In all circumstances, consumption remains omnipresent. Therefore, the question of how to make sense of the conspicuous consumption of those who neither belong to the upper class nor the middle class in South Africa remains.

Aspiration and consumption

There is a unique link between the aspirations that people have and the consumption decisions that they make. Consumption may be a representation of the aspirations that people have (Mnisi 2015). In this sense, *izikhothane*'s consumption is partly a representation or expression of their desires and aspirations. Douglas and Isherwood (1979: 11) argue that consumption is not just an activity of randomly acquiring goods and services but one patterned in specific ways. This means that a range of factors that may include but are not limited to economic factors, cultural background, social circumstances and gender identities inform the overtly observable patterns of human consumption (Mnisi 2015: 23).

Poor people in low-income countries tend to engage more in extravagant consumption against the dictates of rational consumption, suggesting that if you are poor, you are most likely to consume to survive and not show off by creating an identity of wealth (Mnisi 2015). Scholars who have conducted research in low-income countries and made this same deduction include Lamont and Molnar (2001), Banerjee and Duflo (2007), Kaus (2010) and Moav and Neeman (2010).

I argue that the group of *izikhothane* from Daveyton engages in aspirational consumption, which refers to consumption behaviour that represents the aspirations of those who engage in it. Aspirational consumption refers to the goods and services they would consume if they reached a certain level of success. Irrespective of how they may define success in their context, this type of consumption represents a better life.

Dana Goodyear[1] first used the concepts of aspiration and consumption in an article in 2009 about Fred Franzia's success in selling inexpensive wine. The article did not provide a clear definition of this portmanteau of words. I combined the two terms, aspiration and consumption, for my purposes. In my usage, aspirational consumption is consumption with a purpose beyond what is seen (Godelnik 2012).

As a new concept, other writers have taken time to make sense of the consumption patterns of the poor through the avenue of aspiration. Much of the research on aspirational consumption is emerging from studies conducted in India and largely framed within the discourse of the BoP. For instance, Srivastava et al. (2021) define aspirational consumption as inspired by the consumption patterns of those who belong to the upper economic strata of society. Srivastava et al. credit this type of consumption to an internal aspiration to possess the same goods that the wealthy possess in society. According to Srivastava et al. (2021: 1), aspirational consumption 'represents a consumption pattern wherein resource-constrained people yearn to emulate their counterparts who are "better off" in the economic echelons by availing of similar goods and services'. Essentially, at the heart of aspirational consumption is the understanding that the consumer patterns of those stationed at the bottom of the economic pyramid may, at times, exhibit a behaviour of aspiration.

The closest concept to aspirational consumption is aspirational brand. An aspirational brand symbolises wealth (Spacey, 2017) and carries a high premium. Many people desire aspirational brands because of what they represent, but their high prices may discourage some. Therefore, people are more likely to buy these brands when their income increases. In this sense, when people strive to consume aspirational brands without necessarily experiencing a rise in their income, their consumption becomes aspirational as they are consuming the representation of the brand more than the brand itself. Essentially, aspirational consumers are materialists who partly define themselves through brands. Evidently, people's consumption patterns not only represent their cultural values (Lury 1996) but also their aspirations and dreams. In the case of *izikhothane*, they aspire to a better quality of life. More specifically, the consumption patterns of *izikhothane* represent their aspirations to escape poverty and conditions of deprivation and ultimately to become successful according to hegemonic societal norms. These aspirations are evident in the brands they consider to be 'cool', which generate a high social status that would normally be generated by wealth. The consumption of status-generating products is imperative in the act of suggesting the presence of wealth; failure to do so would imply an absence of that wealth, resulting in a low social status (Veblen 1899/2003).

Aspirational consumption is, therefore, different from status consumption. Status consumption is any consumption with the intent of showing off wealth to others, especially when the consumption of goods takes place in public (Scheetz n.d.). The broader body of literature seems to agree with the concept of status consumption, beginning with Veblen's theory of the leisure class, which introduced the concept of conspicuous consumption in the nineteenth century.

Like conspicuous consumption, status consumption is intended to draw attention to present wealth, that is, putting the wealth in evidence to generate a high social status among an individual's reference group (Gumede 2011; Scheetz n.d.; Veblen 1899/2003). Literature documenting conspicuous consumption – the acquisition and display of expensive items to attract attention to one's wealth, as Veblen indicates – or the study of 'bling lifestyles' among black communities refers to status consumption as being intended to communicate the idea that one has 'made it' (Gumede 2011). People engage in conspicuous consumption or status consumption to draw attention to the wealth that is in existence; as such, they put their wealth in evidence.

Aspirational consumption is distinct from status consumption and conspicuous consumption in the sense that aspirational consumption is an extension of the latter. While conspicuous consumption and status consumption imply that wealth exists, with aspirational consumption, wealth does not exist, and this is known to the community. Thus, the outward intention of aspirational consumption is to give the impression that wealth exists even though it is known not to exist. Those who engage in aspirational consumption do not do so to draw attention to their wealth since they have none. Rather, they do so with the implied intention of displaying a desired wealth. It is well known that *izikhothane* do not possess any wealth. Hence, their consumption becomes different in intent from conspicuous and status consumption.

The different forms of consumption are similar in the sense that they are aimed at generating a high social status but differ in their end result: that is, the perceptions that individuals/reference groups have at the end of the signalling. When a rich person engages in conspicuous consumption, observers get the impression that the person is wealthy. On the other hand, when *izikhothane*, who are known to be poor, engage in conspicuous consumption, the common perception is that they are wasteful and not wealthy.

I argue, however, that the consumption patterns of *izikhothane* represent aspirations. The burning that characterises *ukukhothana* should be read literally and figuratively. Literally, a good is set alight and perishes by fire to momentarily elevate the social status of *izikhothane* among their peers; and figuratively, the burning is representative of their intense desire to live an opulent lifestyle. Therefore, their consumption is taken to mean that they aspire to be different, to be wealthy.

Thus far, I have established that how the poor in society consume cannot simply be reduced to conspicuous consumption. Srivastava et al. (2021) discuss the triggers of aspirational consumption, which this section will explore. Figure 6.1 adapts a framework proposed by Srivastava et al. (2021) to delineate the motivations or triggers of the aspirational consumption of the BoP:

Figure 6.1 *Proposed framework of BoP aspirational consumption*

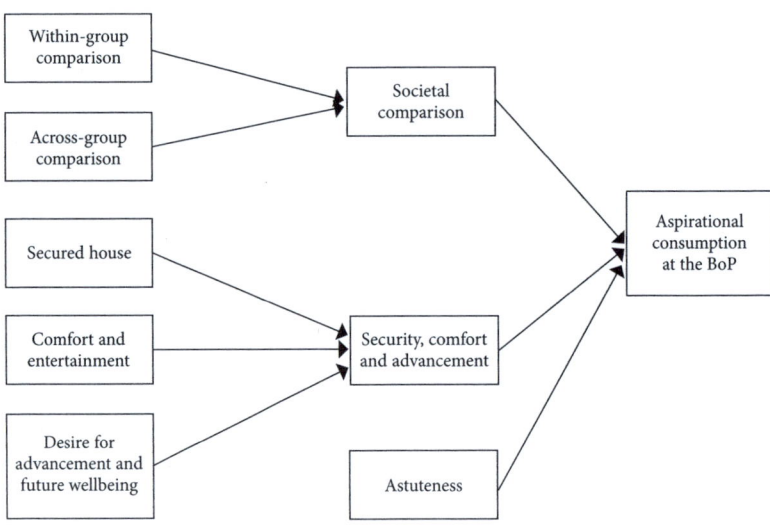

Source: Adapted from Srivastava et al. (2021)

While the list of motivations or triggers of aspirational consumption presented in Figure 6.1 is not exhaustive, it is extensive and contextual.

The first motivation is societal comparison, which highlights how purchasing decisions are made based on comparing oneself to others in society. This includes effectively utilising a social barometer to determine what to consume and its effects on one's social status. The comparison happens at two levels: among those on your level and with those above you in the economic echelons.

For example, in the case of The Good Fellas in Thembisa, there is a large shopping mall called Birch Acres, which boasts fast-food restaurants such as KFC and Debonairs Pizza, and a range of clothing shops, including Truworths, Markham and Total Sports. These shops are significant because they sell some of the brand clothes that The Good Fellas wear, even though the findings indicate that they claim that they do not buy their clothes in these shops because they are within proximity. They prefer clothes from shops that are not within proximity. They call these clothes '*ama*can't get', which means 'difficult to find'. For The Good Fellas, there is something inherently special about things that are rare or difficult to get. This brings to light William Bloke Modisane's words in *Blame Me on History* (1963), which describe the 'Jewish'[2] well-dressed men of Sophiatown, who were exclusively styled with American and English labels unobtainable in Johannesburg. The rarity or, as The Good Fellas say, the 'can't get' element of the clothes makes them more valuable compared to easily accessible ones that are common.

The decision to travel for longer, thus spending more money and time to go to a shopping mall, adds to the notion of conspicuous consumption, particularly Veblen's conspicuous leisure, which is evident in the waste of time. This is not unique to The Good Fellas. Chase et al. (2010) note that about 44 per cent of black South Africans, especially those who live in impoverished conditions, tend to spend more than 15 minutes of travel time to access shopping facilities. While for most poor South Africans, this might be dictated by the absence of shopping facilities near their homes, for The Good Fellas, this is a choice. Most consumers probably regard, for example, Nike sneakers the same, regardless of where they have bought them – whether Thembisa or Johannesburg. However, The Good Fellas believe that distance increases authenticity.

The 'can't get' element of the clothes pushes up the dial on the social barometer of The Good Fellas. On the one hand, societal comparison among the reference group of The Good Fellas is dealt with through shopping outside the immediate community shopping space. On the other hand, shopping at a distance means pursuing consumption in a space that is economically far removed from them and physically inhabited by those stationed above them, economically. Their deliberate entrance into this space is symbolic: they also inhabit a space uniquely encapsulating the promise of a new South Africa and a better life for all.

Another motivation for aspirational consumption is security, comfort and advancement. Interestingly, the pyramid of consumption resembles Abraham Maslow's (1943) hierarchy of needs. Maslow argues that humans are motivated by five basic needs, ranked in order of importance and priority. The needs at the pyramid's base are the most important, and those at the tip are the least important as part of ascendency or mobility. At the base are physiological needs for air, food, water, shelter and sleep. The second need is safety, which involves the pursuit of personal security. The third need is love and belonging. The fourth is esteem, which includes respect from others, self-esteem recognition, and freedom. The last is the need for self-actualisation.

Based on the original thesis of Maslow's hierarchy of needs, I propose a counter-narrative or reading of the classification of needs. From the perspective of those in the BoP segment of consumption, Maslow's pyramid would need to be inverted, with the higher-order needs of self-actualisation forming the BoP and vice-versa.

I locate this argument in the context of South Africa's colonial and apartheid history. Colonialism and apartheid complicated the pursuit of needs in South Africa because they were essentially a project to reduce black people to a subhuman standard. Geographic and social displacement created people with a self-perception of being subhuman. Essentially, black people were taught to remain as nothing more than 'hewers of wood and drawers of water' as promised by Hendrik Verwoerd,[4] South African prime minister under the National Party government in 1958 and a chief proponent of apartheid. His belief was essentially that blacks should never become more than servants of the white minority regime. Posel (2010: 166) elegantly encapsulates this notion:

> That most black people were poor and ill-educated, their bodies typically clad in the garb of poverty, and their interactions unmannered (by European standards) offered circular confirmation of this racial common sense: racial differences were hierarchically constituted in accordance with hierarchies of social status and standing. And in this self-confirming discourse, material possessions and their display (in the first instance, on the body) were crucial pieces of evidence for racial classification.

Posel (2010) speaks to the idea of racial reclassification, referencing a provision made in the 1936 Representation of Natives Act. The Act allowed for certain 'privileges' such as voting. Of interest in this book is the provision for black males to petition the Minister of the Interior to consider them for racial reclassification. Posel notes that they could petition the Minister to classify them as 'non-native' on the grounds of being 'a person of repute'. The requirement was that they should not exhibit traits associated with other 'natives'; in character, they had to be European. This, of course, meant to be clad in sophistication and exhibit a detachment from those 'lacking in social distinction afforded by material ownership and display' (Posel 2010: 166).

Taking the notion of dehumanisation and reading it from the angle of rehumanisation through consumption, as discussed in chapter four, makes the argument of an inverted pyramid of Maslow's hierarchy of needs plausible. Being dehumanised by being reduced to the standard of subhuman could also mean a likelihood of being preoccupied primarily (at the bottom of the pyramid) with the need for self-actualisation and, therefore, seeking rehumanisation. When this first need is achieved, the second need for respect, self-esteem and recognition kicks in. This is done to attain the third need, belonging and love. There is a need to belong to humanity – stripped during the dehumanising project of colonialism. Further, there is also the need to belong to an honourable class, gain prestige, and become a subject of respect, at least in the consumer class. This enables the establishment of friendships and intimacy. Thus, consumption is a criterion to consider. In an interview conducted in Phumulong, Snamzo explicitly remarked:

> Being a *s'khothane* is a competition – you see, we have to let our clothes do the talking. They must tell people that we have money so they can respect us. We know that in reality we don't have money, boss, we are just guys who hustle in order to be respected as real men ... but during our performance we are wealthy. Full stop!

Safety and physiological needs follow last in this pyramid. The need to feel safe is a great one; however, if you have lived in a township where gunshots on the streets are commonplace, and robberies frequent, you somehow tend to learn to live with it. An improved life means leaving the township. Only once one has actualised the self, developed the necessary esteem, and joined the requisite social grouping are safety and essential physiological needs pursued.

The desire to leave the township as a symbol of success was reiterated several times during interviews with The Good Fellas, for example:

> Going forward, my dream is to live *njenge ngamla* [literally, live like a white man; figuratively, live a comfortable life]. I wish to one day leave the township and go and stay in the suburbs with white people and enjoy money because that is where the life is, to be honest, man. The township has a tendency of just condemning one's mind because there are no opportunities here and there are no role models as well. Most of the time we have to inspire ourselves and imagine lives that we do not immediately see. So as soon as I make it financially, I am out of here. But for now, I will dress well and try and enjoy what I have as a young man and imagine the life I want. (Sanego aka Newos)

> Once some people become successful, you see them moving to areas like Midrand, Birchleigh or Edenvale because this place then becomes dangerous for you, man. You move to the suburbs. (Snamzo)

You see, *grootman* [older brother], *la ekasi* [in the location] most people do not make it out because the environment is just too toxic and not conducive for success. There is a lot of crime and drugs. Many people come from prison and they have a backward mentality. (Man-E)

The next trigger is the desire for comfort and entertainment. This brings memories of the popular Afro-pop song by Nomfundo Moh titled 'Soft Life'. The song is about knocking on doors that should be open because of the need for a 'soft life'. The colloquial term 'soft life' has become popularised on social media to mean living a desirable life and accessing all the good things brought forth by wealth, such as comfort and entertainment. While entertainment may be costly, studies cited previously indicate that the BoP segment of the population prioritises it and may overspend on liquor and tobacco products (Kaus 2010; Mnisi 2015; Moav & Neeman 2010).

The most flawed assumption about the BoP population is that they are present-focused and not future-oriented. Reference groups tend to fixate on the 'wasteful' expenditure of this population, spending their limited income on costly present-focused consumption. However, this is visible only on the surface, hence the need for deeper and more focused analyses. This class aspires to live a better life and has dreams often expressed or performed through consumption, enabling the enactment of desired identities.

Snamzo stated:

I'm currently in Grade 11. Next year I'll be finishing school and after that university follows immediately. I want to go to UJ [University of Johannesburg]. I'm not sure about what I want to study but one thing for sure I want to get a good office job and a wear a tie to work.

Snamzo's statement demonstrates a desire to live a better life, achieved through education. Also, parents of The Good Fellas have always supported their children through education and spoke of how they wanted more and better for them. In earlier conversations with

Mpho (Sekatana)'s mother for example, she would ask me to provide guidance on career choices and how to be a good and responsible man. Of course, this did not suggest that I was a perfect or a good man, but I had walked and continue to walk the journey of ambition, development and growth as a black South African man raised by a single domestic worker. On this level, we could identify with each other.

The parents of The Good Fellas continued to demonstrate astuteness as they propelled their children towards attaining education as the 'key to success'. This is evident from how they have made means to keep their sons at school despite some of them being playful and not academically inclined. For example, Sihle aka Bob states:

> I am currently doing Grade 11. Ideally, I should have my matric already, but I dropped out of my previous school. The school that I went to was a private school in Ivory Park for black people and the school fees was R900 monthly – eish, you know, man, black people love money. It became too expensive for my mother since I wasn't doing well, so we agreed that I should go to another school, a cheaper one. I failed because I was very playful, man, and I dance a lot. Being a s'khothane contributed greatly to this. But now I am currently at a night school trying to complete my studies there.

This has been the case with other group members such as Sibusiso aka Mokongoana, who managed to complete college with the support of his mother and attain a Diploma in Public Relations. Similarly, Rabbi noted during one interview:

> My mother works for a logistics company but I am not sure what it is that she does, but I know she is always on her laptop. By the way, she recently graduated with a diploma in something. She inspires me. That is why I also want to make sure that I finish my studies and get a good office job. I can't stand doing hard labour.

Evidently, there is great astuteness that is often missed when observing the consumption patterns of the BoP segment of the population.

This clearly indicates that the narrative that *izikhothane* have only a superficial preoccupation with the present life, and that their thoughts and behaviour are limited to conspicuous consumption at the cost of possible future life enhancement is erroneous. Equally, the expectation that the poor should consume solely for sustenance is an error and takes away their sense of agency and autonomy. This expectation does more to limit their aspirations than any inherent wastefulness in consumption. It is a superficial and shallow perception that seeks to excuse and justify the marginalisation of the poor in the political, economic and social realms.

This narrative is supported by the present government whose focus is on satisfying the longing and hunger for equality in the country. It is appalling that Sandton, considered the richest square mile in Africa, is next to Alexandra, one of the poorest and most densely populated townships in South Africa. Vusimuzi, an informal settlement, is next to Birch Acres; Primrose is next to Makaus in Germiston; Lake Michelle is next to Masiphumelele in Cape Town (ironically, the word masiphumelele means 'let us succeed'); Fourways is next to Diepsloot; Phumulong is next to Midrand. These examples of wealth juxtaposed against poverty demonstrate the glaring levels of socioeconomic inequality in South Africa and the potential role of aspirational consumption in the performance of identities.

Notes

1 Ngcongo M, and Mnisi S (2023). *Izikhothane*: a deeper history of a South African youth subculture where luxury items are trashed. *Daily Maverick*. Available from: https://www.dailymaverick.co.za/article/2023-10-31-izikhothane-a-deeper-history-of-a-south-african-youth-subculture-where-luxury-items-are-trashed/?utm_source=chatgpt.com; Morris A, & Padayachee V (2017). South Africa's youth cultures and the economy of excess. *South African Review of Sociology*, 48(1) 113-130.

2 Goodyear D (2009) Drink up: The rise of really cheap wine. *The New Yorker*, https://www.newyorker.com/magazine/2009/05/18/drink-up

3 Dressing well was known as 'Jewishing' because of how active Jews were seen to be in the South African clothing industry; especially in high-end fashion and quality clothing. As a result, wearing nice clothes came to be associated with being 'Jewish'.

4   Nkomo M (2021) Verwoerd's dream of black people as hewers of wood and drawers of water has become our nightmare. *Daily Maverick* January 13, https://www.dailymaverick.co.za/opinionista/2021-01-13-hendrik-verwoerds-dream-of-black-people-as-hewers-of-wood-and-drawers-of-water-has-become-our-nightmare/

7 On gender performativity: Masculinities and social psychology

When trying to make sense of human behaviour, one realises that a unique and intricate web of social, economic and biological factors intersect and influence how people present themselves. Dissecting each fundamental factor that influences individual presentation offers the opportunity to move towards a more holistic understanding of the being and its behaviour. The social factors speak to the social environment that we exist within and include how we relate to each other as a result of our histories, aspirations, cultures, religious or spiritual beliefs, politics and just about anything to do with our interactions with our environment. The economic factors refer to how demand and supply impact us as they operate in the markets and, in turn, affect our means of living and life-making endeavours. Finally, biological factors speak to how 'nature' interacts with 'nurture' to make sense of life at both a microcosm and macrocosm, and we negotiate nurture and nature to make sense of ourselves.

To make sense of this intricate web that influences how we present ourselves, in this chapter, I want to use three important theories or concepts to form a frame of reference for understanding the behaviour of The Good Fellas and their pursuit of masculinity. This frame of reference draws from the work of Judith Butler on the theory of performativity, the concept of conspicuous consumption and social psychology.

Performativity

The idea of gender as performance is largely espoused by renowned American philosopher and gender studies scholar Judith Butler. Butler (2011) contends that gender is fundamentally a study of 'doing' instead of 'being'. When we study doing as opposed to being, we are essentially studying performances, fleeting acts with deeply engraved social meaning and significance. These performances are executed through the body. Butler interestingly collapses the distinction between sex and gender into one, stating that there is no sex that is not already gendered. The claim here is that all bodies (the natural 'sexed' bodies) are gendered through their social existence (and all existence is social). Gender as a performance then becomes a process of repeated acts 'that take place within a highly regulated social framework' (Butler 2011). Butler (1990) argues that the gender act that one performs exists before the actor – that is, the deed exists before the doer, so it is an act that has been ongoing before one arrives at the scene. Thus, gender is a repetition of stylised acts that involve impersonating an ideal that no one ever really inhabits (Butler 1990).

In looking at gender from the perspective of performativity, it becomes necessary to look at performativity in conjunction with fantasy. This means that gender is more of an act of becoming than a construct of being. Elsewhere, following Simone Beauvoir (1974), Butler argues that the state of being a man or woman is a historical fact. The habitation of this physiological body compels the body to conform to the historical idea of what it means to be a man or a woman (Butler 1990). As such, when we call ourselves men or women, we essentially enact a historical sense of being as we perform that identity.

In effect, gender is so silent that what we refer to as gender identity is a performative accomplishment that results from a complex interplay of social sanctions and taboos. Essentially, the suggestion is that there is nothing natural about gender as a social construct. People can become whatever they desire. The only caveat is the social sanctions and taboos associated with the enacted identity. Naturalised expectations, therefore, guide behaviour. Furthermore, the performance of gender identity may be so extreme that people put themselves in danger through a myriad of risky and compromising behaviours in an attempt to inhabit the gender ideal.

Locating conspicuous consumption in social psychology

A body of theory and research locates conspicuous consumption in evolutionary biology, suggesting that conspicuous consumption may have evolved as a sexually selected mating tactic (see Griskevicius et al. 2007; Saad & Vongas 2009). Research that locates consumption in evolution often draws from the work of Charles Darwin (1859) on sexual selection, a subset of natural selection that looks at the preference for mating partners with qualities that may increase the likelihood of survival (Zahavi 1975).

Sexual selection seeks to make sense of a puzzle in the animal kingdom when females select male mating partners. The males' attractive signalling features paradoxically threaten their possibility of survival. An example is the gloriously conspicuous feathers of a peacock, which attract the attention of a peahen. As useful as this signalling is, it is very costly as it hinders movement and dangerously exposes the peacock to predators. Zahavi (1975) explains this costly signalling through the 'handicap' principle, which suggests that by exposing oneself to the pressures of natural selection in a manner that is detrimental to survival – that is, by handicapping oneself – and emerging unharmed, one proves worthiness for mating. Thus, the ability to emerge unharmed from signalling renders the peacock a worthy mating partner, as it can withstand a hazardous environment.

However, as Zahavi (1975) notes, Darwin could not explain why this conspicuous display was mainly inherent in males rather than females. In 1972, the American evolutionary biologist and sociologist Robert Trivers coined the concept of 'parental investment' to explain the apparent conundrum in Darwin's theory. Parental investment refers to the minimum investment each parent makes in reproducing an offspring (Griskevicius et al. 2007: 665). The concept holds that males (including human beings) invest minimally in the production of offspring in terms of the time and energy that it takes to have sexual intercourse. On the other hand, female investment is greater because females render more time and energy for internal gestation and nursing of the offspring (Griskevicius et al. 2007: 655). The conclusion is, therefore, that the gender with a greater investment in the production of offspring is choosier than the counterpart, whose investment is less. The result is that the male species possessing the conspicuous traits signals, while the female chooses the best mating partner.

Griskevicius et al. (2007) note that this pattern has been documented across a wide range of species, including human beings. Accordingly, 'conspicuous consumption represents an adaptive communication strategy aimed at obtaining reproductive rewards' (Griskevicius et al. 2007: 675).

Looking at the work that has been done on sexual selection, costly signalling and parental investment, the implication is that conspicuous consumption in people may possibly serve the same purpose as the feathers of a peacock. People attempt to publicly handicap themselves with a financial burden to send a reliable signal about their socioeconomic status to their peers. My interest is in these signals as men convey them. However, the logic of conspicuous consumption must not be used as an essentialist understanding of men as a homogenous group. Rather, gendered identities are made of heterogeneous individuals who behave uniquely in various contexts.

There are contexts in which certain men exhibit the handicap and thus for whom conspicuous consumption may be a sexually selected mating tactic. In the sample that formed part of the study conducted by Griskevicius et al. (2007), men engaged in conspicuous consumption to establish a short-term relationship. Following Richards' (2015) and Mkhwanazi's (2011) observations about how the participants in their respective research use conspicuous consumption to impress girls, the same logic may be reached in understanding the behaviour of *izikhothane*. *Izikhothane* is known to use conspicuous consumption to gain access to women and sex. *Izikhothane* even go to the extent of buying alcohol for the women that they seek to impress, hoping that this will potentially lead to sexual intercourse.

A couple of things become clear in these circumstances. Given the fact that *izikhothane* come from impoverished socioeconomic backgrounds, engaging in conspicuous consumption is a handicap because it places a costly financial burden on them. Further, the financial burden means sacrificing other things, such as contributing to their homes. Another observation is the nature of relationships formed in this context, which have a very short life span, often lasting for no longer than one night. *Izikhothane* hypocritically note that they would not even consider marrying the girls that they sleep with, as they are supposedly not 'wife material' because of their obsession with material things and the nightlife.

The signal that comes from men has cultural significance within a patriarchal context where reference is often made to men as 'providers', and that emphasises economic achievement by men, therefore making such men viable partners. In this context, the ability to provide becomes key in making men viable mating partners as they are assumed to have the ability to invest materially.

Applying the idea of conspicuous consumption as a sexual selection tactic seems relevant to the logic behind *izikhothane* behaviour. However, two considerations muddy the waters here. Firstly, short-term relationships may not always lead to the reproduction of offspring. Griskevicius et al. (2007) explain that the nature of the relationship is meant to be without any strings attached, a short romantic fling. The focus is on the sexual act that results from the signalling, not on reproduction. In the case of *izikhothane*, they 'get their girls' whom they 'will not marry'. How do we make sense of this? The second consideration is about the validity of the signal, or what Zahavi (1975) calls 'honest signalling', which begs the question of honesty in the signalling of *izikhothane*, since they are not necessarily as wealthy as they portray themselves to be. An argument that could be made is that the value of the signal remains valid, as it achieves the intended outcome – a 'short-term, romantic fling' – and what happens afterwards, or the individual's socioeconomic status, becomes a different conversation.

A big handi-'cap': Making sense of signalling and multiple sexual partners through social psychology

In soccer, the concept of a cap describes the number of times a player has played international matches for his national team.[1] This old tradition originates from the United Kingdom, in which players were awarded actual caps for their first international game. Over the years, as the tradition spread to other nations and various sporting codes, it came to mean a number instead of a physical cap that a player receives. Each international match a player participates in and represents their country earns them a single cap. Therefore, the more caps a player receives, the more honour they receive because it means they are good at what they do, and the nation can rely on them for good representation. Many caps represent prestige. The words 'cap' and 'player' cannot be separated literally or figuratively – both on the field, which would be the literal sense, and off the field in the figurative sense.

The concept of a 'player' has also done the rounds off the soccer pitch and is associated with earning 'caps' in the dating game. Though there are many definitions of what a 'player' is in dating, consensus exists that this person dates multiple partners and is generally not interested in committing to a relationship yet could make the other party believe that they are committed (Frost 2018). According to Frost (2018), players 'are usually charming and may sweep you off your feet with their romantic talk and gestures'. The term 'gesture' refers to a communicative signal from which inferences about someone's intentions can be made. The recipient of the message can draw conclusions from the communication and decide whether to indulge or ignore the communicator.

The gesturing characteristic of players could be understood in terms of Zahavi's (1975) concept of the handicap principle, described earlier, in making sense of sexual selection in the animal kingdom. I know that comparing animals' behaviours to humans may be problematic. However, doing so in this case serves as an analogy. For example, when The Good Fellas praise a member who has done well or is good at doing something or has achieved something, they refer to him as *inkunzi*. *Inkunzi* is an isiZulu word for a bull, known for its strength and sexual reproduction or mating capacity, sheer size, physical strength and territorial domination over cows within a herd. Often in isiZulu, when a man is praised for being great at something, he is referred to as *inkunzi emnyama*, which directly translates to 'black bull' – believed to be especially strong – and such a reference carries a lot of honour and shows respect. Therefore, in this sense, I deem the use of animals to describe certain behaviours in humans, particularly in men, not offensive and justified to make a point.

In this context, the handicap principle has found its way into descriptions of human behaviour. Griskevicius et al. (2011) postulate that conspicuous consumption among people may serve the handicapping function of a peacock's tail. Al-Shawaf and Lewis (2017) extend this idea by noting that the act of conspicuous consumption places a financial burden on people, which, in a sense, publicly handicaps them as they do this to signal their socioeconomic status to their reference group. A relevant example that would demonstrate how this works among The Good Fellas is evident from a conversation that I had with Vega who explained:

> During the mock battle, man, you must be ready for anything. For example, a guy can just be dancing then come to you and tear your T-shirt from the neck down, and you can't fight him because doing that means you can't really afford to be a *s'khothane*, you are simply claiming *nje* [just], you are not a real man.

Clearly, in this instance, the contestant is publicly handicapping himself. He, therefore, must present an image to his peers that he has not been 'harmed' or suffered any loss, because whatever he has lost does not matter as he supposedly has more and can afford the loss. When conspicuous consumption as a handicap functions as a sexually selected mating tactic, it is usually for an uncommitted relationship that tends to end after sex (Griskevicius et. al. 2011). In this sense, conspicuous consumption becomes a strategy aimed at securing sexual intercourse. In Chapter 4, Skopo makes it clear that he is not interested in long-term relationships. Indeed, how could one have long-term relationships with nine women – unless one is a polygamist? And we know that this is not the case here, because Skopo says he is doing this only because he is young. Sihle, aka Bob, expands this idea below in an extract from an interview:

> So, when I need to buy clothes ... I start saving up. My mother always adds to my savings, so I can go buy the clothes that I want. When I have my clothes on, I bring my A-game to the dance floor. Bro, women go crazy! I don't want to lie to you, man, I love girls. As we speak, I have four girlfriends. I think they are attracted to me by my dance

and clothes. They also love my name, Bob, it is a cool name, so it also attracts them. And *ngiyazibhuncula* [I have sex with them]. I mean managing these women is not difficult because they all know each other ... I am not a polygamist, and I will only marry one woman.

Bob makes it clear that buying expensive clothes is not easy as it requires him not only to save but for his mother to also step in to supplement his savings. He explains above that his dance moves and conspicuous consumption make girls go 'crazy': they make him attractive and thereby able to access these girls sexually.

Another aspect of the idea of sexual selection through conspicuous consumption is the resultant reproductive rights. There is a strong possibility of the emergence of offspring because the presentation indicates money, which suggests the ability to take care of the woman and an unfounded illusion of 'security'. This supposedly makes the man attractive to the girls. Vega is a good example of this as he has a child born from a mother that he met at an *izikhothane* event. He explained:

> Yes ... man, I have a kid now and I must be responsible, and I can't be doing as I please. She is a beautiful baby girl who was born a month ago. I love the mother of my child as well. I think she is a good investment, you know. Academically she is doing well. She knows when she must be at home (she stays with her paternal grandmother). We [met] during my days of *ukukhothana*.

Figure 7.1 *Vega and his family*

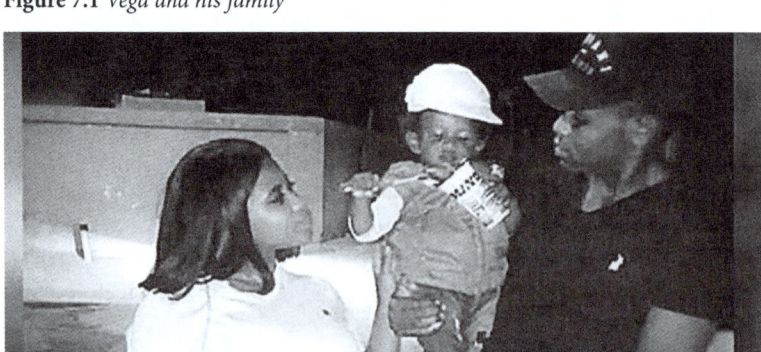

Source: Image supplied by author.

The handicap principle, which I apply to conspicuous consumption, helps make sense of the behaviour of The Good Fellas. However, it does not explain a relationship that began as the result of the handicap principle and not only creates an offspring but then becomes long-term, with future aspirations of turning the woman into a lifelong partner because 'she is wife material'. Though the handicap might start the relationship, it does not sustain it. While the presentation of a handicap has the potential of increasing the number of caps for the player, the handicap principle does not consider the longevity of romantic relationships.

The screenshot on the previous page shows how Vega already refers to his daughter and girlfriend as 'family'. However, another aspect that needs consideration here is the fact that the pregnancy was not deliberate and adds to the concerning scourge of teenage pregnancies that the Miss Masakhane Beauty Pageant is fighting.[2] This is a contradiction because Vega is an avid participant in this initiative. As such, it becomes clear that additional information beyond signalling may either sustain a relationship or end it.

Through the handicap

The concept of mating is often used to refer to sexual relations as they occur among animals for procreation. In this sense, using this term to describe people's behaviour carries some negative connotations. Further, mating in the animal kingdom is specifically associated with procreation. However, in borrowing from the animal kingdom, social psychology has us realising that we could successfully look at it to make sense of some aspects of human behaviour. In this case, conspicuous consumption, which appears to have evolved as a sexually selected mating strategy (Griskevicius et al. 2011), helps explain the behaviour of The Good Fellas. It is, however, important to note that people do not have sexual relations only for procreation but also for recreational, romantic and other purposes. This is evident in the fact that people have developed strategies, contraceptives and techniques for having sex without procreating. These are methods that The Good Fellas often use to try and prevent procreation and limit sexual intercourse to recreation, which is also a strategy to earn them respect among their peers and to be considered 'men'. To reiterate a point raised earlier, being a *s'khothane* is associated with having plenty of sexual experiences and knowing about sexual protection and contraception.

Apart from preventing unplanned pregnancy while having sex, contraception is also used to prevent sexually transmitted diseases. Mthigo's reference to 'looking like a skeleton' (Chapter 4) refers to contracting the Human Immunodeficiency Virus (HIV) and the subsequent development of Acquired Immune Deficiency Syndrome (AIDS), whose symptoms include rapid weight loss. This concern has validity in the South African context, given that the estimation of people living with HIV was 7.8 million in 2023, with youths between 15 and 24 years of age accounting for many of these infections.[3]

The pursuit of recreational sex is more prevalent among people who tend to be active in clubs at night (Ludden 2019). Ludden cites a study by Kasaeian and his colleagues at Tubingen University, which documents the relationship between sex and chronotype (an individual's variation in alertness and activity during the hours of the day/night). The study suggests that people who have an active nightlife, such as going to nightclubs, tend to engage more in casual sex and are generally open to short-term relationships. They usually have more sexual partners in their lifetime than those who do not have an active nightlife.

Interestingly, though, the study notes that those who are active at night and have more frequent sex have fewer children than those not in this category. The Good Fellas fit the category of having an active nightlife and more sexual partners, but without having more children. For them, engagement in sex is also linked to a sense of accomplishment – so much so that those among them who are not sexually active are considered to be weak and are often ridiculed. Vega alludes to this:

> Even if we go out and you come back without a girl for a one-night stand, we would laugh at you because it means you don't get the concept of rush hours (when pubs are about to close guys usually stay close to their girls so that

they don't disappear or get taken by other guys). Or if
you no longer get one-night stands, we'll tell you that
you are weak.

'Rush hours' refers to post-midnight hours when pubs are about to close. Vega explains that every member must ensure they have a woman they will spend the night with before the pub closes, as this is when most men seek to secure a woman for a one-night stand. Those who fail to secure a woman become objects of scorn in the group. This speaks to the importance of sex in the performance of masculinity among the members of the group. Engaging in masturbation is something to be ashamed of. Multiple sexual partners are something to be proud of, as Snamzo alludes to below:

> Staying with my grandmother, as a man, I feel that it gives
> me the freedom I need because at this age, now and then,
> I need to sneak in a different girl home. Now imagine if
> I had to do that staying with my parents in a room inside
> the house. Or having to return home from a night of heavy
> partying at the crack of dawn. My mother would never
> allow that.

This detour into explaining the relationship between sex and chronotype is useful. However, for us to conclude that those who have more sex, in general, have fewer babies would be problematic – especially if we were to apply the same logic to the whole of Tembisa, given concerns about the alarming rise in teenage pregnancies. However, as noted by the Department of Health, most teenage pregnancies were a result of suspected transactional relationships with older men taking advantage of young girls.[4] Considering this, The Good Fellas' initiatives to reduce pregnancy rates through their involvement with the annual Miss Masakhane Beauty Pageant could be seen as proof that they are doing their part – despite their night-time activities – with notable exceptions in this regard. Perhaps it is also important to note that there is no evidence of whether those who were part of the surge in teenage pregnancies in Tembisa are active at night or not. The comments here relate solely to observations made by The Good Fellas.

What then of performance, masculinity and the handicap theory? Essentially, the unique intersection of masculinity and Zahavi's (1975) concept of the handicap, Butler's (1990) idea of performativity, and Veblen's (1899) conspicuous consumption paint a compelling picture of how men navigate societal expectations about their gender and how they negotiate their identity. Through this intersection, the notion of masculinity can be viewed as a process of becoming, rather than as a state of being – a constant negotiation between nature and nurture.

Notes

1. What does 'cap' mean in football/soccer? Accessed 22 September 2019, https://www.quora.com/What-does-cap-mean-in-football-soccer
2. The annual Miss Masakhane Beauty Pageant was started by a former Good Fella, Siya, in 2008, as an initiative to help end teenage pregnancies.
3. HSRC (2023) New HIV survey highlights progress and ongoing disparities in South Africa's HIV epidemic. Available from: https://hsrc.ac.za/press-releases/phsb/new-hiv-survey-highlights-progress-and-ongoing-disparities-in-south-africas-hiv-epidemic/
4. 'Sugar daddies' and 'blessers': A threat to Aids fight. Agence France-Presse, 21 Jul 2016. https://www.ndtv.com/world-news/sugar-daddies-and-blessers-a-threat-to-aids-fight-1434140

8 Aspirational masculinities: Consumption, masculinities and being a Good Fella

Does success have 'a race'? A simple answer to this question in the context of post-apartheid South Africa would be 'no'. However, the connections between race and the subsequent references to the symbolism of success are far deeper reaching and call for a more nuanced analytical response. The tools of discourse-historical approach and multimodal critical discourse analysis may provide a deeper understanding of the discourse around race and wealth.

Making sense of everyday discourse

The expressions around how we use language to make sense of wealth or success in relation to race necessitate the acknowledgement that our choice of words is seldom random and often deeply rooted in our perceived social, political and economic hierarchies, both real and imagined. Further, we should acknowledge that our communication is intertwined with social processes of meaning. Thus, we must acknowledge the historical background of seemingly discursive events.

For example, I attained my basic schooling at Zamukhanyo Primary School in Daveyton, a township in the East Rand of Gauteng Province. It is a public school, and most learners come from working-class families. Often, teachers would ask us to stand up and inform the whole class what we wanted to become when we grew up. My classmates would say 'a doctor' or 'a teacher' or 'a police'. One day, a fellow learner made everyone laugh, including our teacher, when he stood up and confidently said: 'I want to be a white man'. We laughed because it was funny, but for a primary school learner to say this was his dream is a revelatory moment for me, especially in my interactions with The Good Fellas. Notably, black people who are considered successful or well accomplished are often referred to as *ingamla* or *umlungu*, which means white person.

In my random conversations with Snamzo, who is a taxi driver, I also noticed that he would often refer to his employer as *umlungu* or *ingamla yam*, which directly translates to 'my white man' meaning 'my boss'. Initially, I was confused and thought that his employer was a white man who stayed in Edenvale because this is where his boss stays. Edenvale is a predominantly white area from which the apartheid government forcefully removed the people of Thembisa. My confusion stemmed from the fact that white people are not typically involved in the taxi industry, which is predominantly owned by black businesspeople. However, I realised the symbolism of the term 'white man' in this context: that it had little to do with race but more with the person's standard of living. The understanding is that a seemingly wealthy person who can employ another, something associated with being white, immediately 'earns' the status of being white. It became clear once again to me how the life of affordability and perhaps even upward mobility was associated with whiteness, and a black person's attainment of wealth was, in a sense, a discursive attainment of whiteness. This perception even extends to specific consumption patterns associated with whiteness, where excess consumption seeks to serve a liberating role.

Symbols of success

Zine Magubane's *Bringing the Empire Home: Race, Class and Gender in Britain and Colonial South Africa* (2004), which addresses the politics of consumption in the colonial era, draws an interesting parallel between the identities of mineworkers in Kimberley around the 1880s and the out-of-work diamond fields dandies of the time. The idea of attaining an identity that the oppressed people were denied, one that transcended servitude, becomes key. Magubane (2004) highlights how money somehow enabled mineworkers to achieve something inconceivable: buying whiteness through consumption. In this sense, the idea was that wearing the clothes of the dandies (initially white and European) transformed the identities of the black mineworkers. Again, it becomes apparent how the racially curtailed class distinctions continue to manifest in our everyday lives and continue to form part of our discourses.

Figure 8.1 Rabbi at his matric farewell party

Source: Image supplied by author.

Similarly, when Rabbi attended his matric farewell (Figure 8.1), his description of the opulence at the gala dinner also alluded to whiteness. He described how they were treated like *amangamla*, meaning white people, and how they ate with a fork and a knife, as white people do. Another member of the group named Enough – who is known in the group as Man Enough or Man-E – also shared his matric farewell story about how they 'ate using a fork and a knife' and how they were 'serious', somehow implying that eating with these utensils made the act of eating more significant. This comment reminded me of the value of utensils in signalling conspicuous consumption and of how silverware signals wealth in Veblen's (1899) *The Theory of the Leisure Class*. Of course, it is different in this case, as I would imagine that in the Rabbi's context, the ability to use these utensils is a symbol of one's social class. Similarly, Anna Trapido (2008) recounts Nelson Mandela's story about his embarrassment when he visited a girl he liked and had dinner with her middle-class family, who ate using a fork and a knife, something unfamiliar to him. As a romantic gesture, the young girl jumped to his rescue by making him feel comfortable about using his hands by dipping her bare hands into her food. This indicates a person's social class, at least among black families in the township, where people generally use their hands or a spoon to eat.

In the summer of 2019, Vega also attended his matric farewell. He and a friend, who has a Volkswagen Polo, drove to the venue with their two dates. On their way, they had a flat tyre, and as the 'men', they assured their female dates that they would sort everything out because it was their responsibility to ensure that they arrived at the venue safely. As promised, they did. Upon arrival at the venue, they changed into formal clothes for the gala dinner. Vega was dazzling in a maroon suit (Figure 8.2) that earned him the fifth position in the best-dressed category. He says he could not clinch the first prize because the person adjudicating the contest was his neighbour, and his winning would have been read as unfair. What struck me about Vega's photos, which he posted on his WhatsApp status, is how he constantly posed with a wine glass. When I asked him about his reason for the poised handling of the glass and how it has become part of his accessory in the pictures, he responded in a voice note with the following:

> You see, grootman, a glass in such situations puts you under a lot of pressure, and you need to know how to hold it because everyone is watching. You can't just be clumsy when handling it. You must also remember that today we are wearing the uniform for this glass and you need to know how to handle it and how to walk with it in your hand. Another thing, when holding this type of glass, you can't be seen pacing up and down ... no man, you need to have a collected walk and be calm, you know, be a classic man. Because the thing about this glass is that it makes you feel special as if you are wealthy and you own a lot of businesses ... You see, when you are holding it like this it changes how people even look at you because they don't know where you come from, so you must walk like you are a millionaire. Like this is something that would make you want to change your life because such things we only see in movies with the bosses walking around with it. So, you need to act likewise.

Figure 8.2 *Vega posing with his glass during the matric farewell ceremony*

Source: Image supplied by author.

How success looks like Ekasi – *in the township*

Another aspect of whiteness that appears to be associated with success is one's residential area. The creation of the township, first through colonialism and later intensified by the apartheid system to be the dwelling place of white people's servants who were only allowed to enter the city as workers with permits and then later leave when their work was complete, shaped The Good Fellas' perceptions. The construction of the township through a process of 'othering' aligned to the ideology of apartheid made it a place of marginality and a place of managed aspirations. As noted by Ellapen (2007: 113), the township represents a 'manageable part of modernity for "black identity"'. As a result of this historical context, some people in townships subconsciously perceive upward mobility as synonymous with vertical mobility to the northern suburbs of Johannesburg or any other suburb that houses white people. The perception is that, by leaving the township, they leave behind the managed black identity. Leaving symbolises autonomy.

This desire to leave the township as a symbol of success was reflected several times during the interviews with The Good Fellas, as noted in the following instances:

> Going forward, my dream is to live *njenge ngamla* [literally, live like a white man; figuratively, live a comfortable life]. I wish to one day leave the township and go and stay in the suburbs with white people and enjoy money because that is where the life is, to be honest, man. The township has a tendency of just condemning one's mind because there are no opportunities here and there are no role models as well. Most of the time we have to inspire ourselves and imagine lives that we do not immediately see. So as soon as I make it financially, I am out of here. But for now, I will dress well and try and enjoy what I have as a young man and imagine the life I want. (Sanego, aka Newos)

> Once some people become successful, you see them moving to areas like Midrand, Birchleigh or Edenvale because this place then becomes dangerous for you, man. You move to the suburbs. (Snamzo)

> You see, grootman, la ekasi most people do not make it out because the environment is just too toxic and not conducive for success. There is a lot of crime and drugs. Many people come from prison and they have a backward mentality. (Man-E)

The three remarks above uniquely capture two perceptions about the township. Firstly, it is a place where people find themselves due to their economic circumstances and not by choice. In a sense, it is a place to leave once one's financial circumstances change. Secondly, crime is rife in the township, and people who remain there after attaining success inadvertently become victims of crime.

Stereotypes depicting the township as a place of poverty and a haven for criminals who roam the streets like lions seeking prey continue to characterise the discourses of success. Similar stereotypical associations of the township are observed by Ellapen (2007), particularly as a place of othering. Whether they raise valid concerns or not, such perceptions continue to perpetuate the stereotypical narrative of this place as 'the other'. As these are the views and aspirations of The Good Fellas, they are not necessarily true for everyone, as many people continue to stay in townships by choice, regardless of their perceptions and their socioeconomic positions. A good example of such a person who remained in the township by choice was the late former wife of Nelson Mandela, Winnie Madikizela-Mandela, who remained in her Orlando West home in Soweto when she could have moved to the suburbs.

The realities and the experiences of people in the township are unique. It would be an error to portray a picture of the township as an environment no one wants to inhabit. Indeed, people who stay in townships are not necessarily unhappy. Among The Good Fellas, they share a feeling that there is something inherently beautiful about the township; they often describe it as a haven of freedom where they can express themselves and be creative in living their lives amid all the challenges. Further, The Good Fellas make an obvious effort to improve and bring about development in their corners. This is evident from their participation in the beauty pageant and an initiative that seeks to fight pollution and promote living in a clean environment through the Rabbi Letageng Youth Foundation (RLYF). (This registered non-profit organisation will be discussed later in this chapter.)

Upward mobility is synonymous with leaving the township

Another element of the perception of whiteness as life outside the township and as success is evinced by Mpho (Sekatana), who feels that he should do his shopping outside the township, for example, by travelling to towns such as Kempton Park and the Johannesburg central business district. Sarah Nuttall's work on youth consumption and mall cultures, particularly her article titled 'Stylizing the Self: The Y Generation in Rosebank, Johannesburg', notes (2004: 431) that in post-1994 South Africa, urban areas are 'critical sites for the remixing and reassembling of racial identities' and observes this specifically in Johannesburg. The city's ability to allow racial remixing underscores the aspirational identities that young people seek. Thus, The Good Fellas' entrance into these urban areas to purchase clothes and take them to the townships to perform their enacted identities speaks to the creativity involved in creating an urban youth culture. This not only highlights their prevailing realities but also their aspirations.

Figure 8.3 *Mpho (Sekatana) and Tshepo walking to Festival Mall in Kempton Park*

Source: Image supplied by author.

Figure 8.3 shows two young men of The Good Fellas accessing a space that subjectively symbolises distinction. Notably, the towns outside of townships often provide facilities for recreation that are not always available in the township. Some of these facilities have come to be associated with upward mobility. This is something to which The Good Fellas aspire, and by inserting themselves in these spaces, the mobility process has already begun. This is like Lury's (1996) idea that through aspiring to be a member of a particular culture, one might be symbolically incorporated into it, as one's actions, goals and desires are more likely to be geared towards attaining perceived status in that culture.

Another unique scenario is the popular Ice Rink at Festival Mall, which attracts The Good Fellas. In 2024, the Festival Mall Ice Rink charged an entrance fee of R80 and another R35 deposit to hire a pair of skates. Clearly, it is not cheap to access this facility if one also considers the taxi fare that must be paid to get to Kempton Park from Thembisa. Bambo, who enjoys ice skating, has mastered it and even performs numerous tricks on the rink, which speaks to how much time and, by extension, money he has spent at this facility. He skates in style, wearing Kappa tracksuit pants and a Raw T-shirt (Figure 8.4), both of which are costly. What is interesting, though, is that Bambo does not only skate but also dances while skating. He does the *kwasa kwasa* dance[1] and other flamboyant *s'khothane* dances while skating. What is also apparent is the creativity with which he infiltrates this space. This is the same creativity that makes it difficult to follow Veblen's and Simmel's model of emulation when people who are at the bottom of the pyramid (BoP) engage in conspicuous consumption, in this case, in the conspicuous leisure and squandering of time by skating. Aspiration is apparent here but certainly not emulation.

Figure 8.4 *Bambo at the Festival Mall Ice Rink*

Source: Image supplied by author.

What is the colour of success?

To revisit the opening question in this chapter: 'Does success have race?', this section will discuss two types or meanings of 'race', drawing from an analogy in Deborah Posel's (2010) seminal article titled 'Races to Consume: Revisiting South Africa's History of Race, Consumption and the Struggle for Freedom'. The first type is the complex and much-debated race that Posel (2010: 161) conceptualises as the 'social construction of bodily difference, practices that have been inseparable from other fault lines of difference and repertoires of power'. In South Africa, the apartheid government introduced four official racial categorisations, which are still widely used today: black, Indian, coloured and white.

The second type of race refers to an act of running to get to a finishing line or a destination, generally as a form of competition. The latter type or meaning is, in this context, used figuratively to describe the act of pursuing success alongside one's peers, which, in a sense, makes it a race that is of interest in this book. The political history of South Africa, which made class, race and consumption synonymous, continues to influence our discourses about issues of social class. The long history of oppression and dehumanisation of the black body, which portrayed white South Africans and their lives as the epitome of civilisation, continues to inform post-apartheid discourses about social class and the complex efforts to rehumanise the black self. Further, these perceptions continue to influence consumption patterns. Therefore, they show that consumption is part of a complex continuum of sociocultural and socioeconomic relations. The complexities of consumption manifest in various facets of the lived experiences of township youths. This is further evidenced in the pursuit and performances of masculinities within the precarious market of township identities.

Aspirational masculinities

To make sense of aspirational masculinities, I want to return to some key concepts discussed: masculinities, townships, consumption, aspiration and BoP segment. Essentially, when I speak about aspirational masculinities, I am referring to the pursuit of a form of masculinity that holds the hegemonic position in society but is merely aspired to in the township context. The pursuit of this masculinity is reliant on the vehicle of consumption. The males who seek to inhabit this identity engage in aspirational consumption. I rely on the concept of aspiration because at the core of this masculine identity spectrum is the desire to be more, to see better, to develop and – most importantly – for all these attributes to be observable to others in society. The situation of *izikhothane* demonstrates the notion of aspiration and the resultant identity of manhood associated with it.

Issues of gender cannot be separated from the activities of *izikhothane* and play a critical role in this subculture. In his fascinating qualitative study *Izikhothane: Masculinity and Class in Katlehong, a South African Township*, James Richards (2015) relies on the constructionist paradigm to investigate *ukukhothana* in Katlehong in the East Rand. Katlehong has a rich history of political contestation and struggle against apartheid. Here, specific kinds of masculinities, characterised by militarised subcultures and structures aimed at resisting the oppressive regime (Langa & Eagle 2008), can be seen as the legacy of this struggle.

There is a belief in *ukukhothana* that manhood is associated with access to financial resources. When put in evidence, financial resources attract women, presumably because women are attracted to men who can provide for them. It suggests that manhood is synonymous with having money and thus being able to access women (Richards 2015: 114). This aligns with Bourdieu's (1986: 17) concept of cultural capital. In the case of *izikhothane*, having cultural capital is an inherent advantage gleaned from having access to specific resources. As such, access to money and popularity gives one access to girls.

Richards reports that *izikhothane* have a sense of ownership of the women as they believe themselves to be the providers. He, however, clarifies that in this context, the term 'provision' specifically relates to these young men's ability to provide alcohol for the women. This gives them the benefits linked with providing, such as consensual sex for example, which to them is a marker of manhood. According to Richards, the participants use their involvement in *ukukhothana* to legitimise their domination of women through their supposed ability to provide. This status justifies their practice of having multiple girlfriends and sexual partners.

The role of the women is to be avid supporters of the men, and they do not have to wear expensive clothes; they must just be beautiful. Unfortunately, without beauty, the females are considered irrelevant or even weaken the group's status, as beauty is the only currency they have working for them (Richards 2015: 117). When female *izikhothane* exist, they merely do so as supporters in the shadows of their male counterparts. They do not engage in the destruction characteristic of the male *izikhothane*.

There is an unfortunate double standard in involving girls in the subculture, which speaks to the commodification of women in pursuit of the hyper-masculinity characteristic of *izikhothane*. Richards (2015: 118) notes that 'in as much as they expect there to be numerous women attending the events and afterwards having sex with them, the women they will ultimately marry are not those who attend *s'khothane* events'. This double standard is rationalised through the patriarchal belief that the 'appropriate' place for a woman is in the kitchen, and those who choose this 'gallivanting' lifestyle become sex objects and are treated as such. The men's disapproval of women's participation in this lifestyle is illustrated in their declaration that they would not allow their daughters to participate (Richards 2015: 119). As Richards observes, boys with several girlfriends are celebrated in the township, while girls with multiple boyfriends are frowned upon.

Ukukhothana is a highly competitive subculture in which dancing better than your opponents, dissing them more, wearing more expensive clothes, or having more girlfriends than they do earns you the crown. Those who claim victory are considered men, and their masculinity reigns over all other masculine identities, something that Connell (1995) refers to as hegemonic masculinity. Richards (2015: 125) observes that when *izikhothane* claim victory, they subsequently position themselves as 'occupying the hegemonic masculinity in their context'. They define other masculinities in derogatory terms to elevate themselves. For example, the participants in Richards' study would refer to other men who do not engage in the subculture or do not have multiple girlfriends as 'boys'. The subculture of *ukukhothana* positions itself above other subcultures, and *izikhothane* consider themselves superior because of the clothes they wear. They claim that other people want to be like them, thus gaining upward social mobility (Richards & Langa 2015: 100–101).

Richards' (2015) findings speak to my 2015 study on another crew of *izikhothane* in Daveyton regarding the definition of a 'man' as linked to financial resources. It also became evident that achieving 'manhood' or a masculine identity is associated with amassing social power. Social power, which can generate honour for individuals (Mnisi 2015: 97), is gained through possessing things that are socially admired, such as economic stability, which may be achieved by having a stable job, a successful business or an education. However, to realise this power, all the factors contributing to its possession must be put in evidence; they need to be seen or heard. The determining factors of the supposed manhood or masculine identity are drawn from the parameters of a patriarchal society built on the foundation of the supremacy of men. However, I also found something intriguing, which other scholars have confirmed in subsequent studies: the element of aspiration.

The middleman: Media representations of masculinities and consumption in South Africa

The media plays a crucial role in people's consumption choices. Specifically focusing on the BoP consumer segment, Nyanga (2015) discusses how this segment is exposed to various media and, as a result, is brand-conscious in its consumption. In the same vein, Prahalad (2012) argues that this market segment is flooded by mediated marketing messages that sell not only products but also lifestyles. The link between the media and the consumption patterns of *izikhothane* is important.

Etymologically, the word 'media' (the plural form of 'medium') is Latin, which refers to the 'middle' ground. Drawing from this, I view the media as institutions that mediate reality and facilitate communication between two or more people (Cope & Kalantzis 2015: 373). Given the pervasiveness of the media in contemporary society, media defines and legitimises certain identities and ways of being and living over others (Malinga & Ratele 2016), including forms of manhood and masculinity. These media representations have immense implications for the consumption patterns of *izikhothane* and the men's idealised sense of self.

In *The System of Objects*, French sociologist Jean Baudrillard (2005) argues that when a person becomes a consumer, they essentially get into a relationship with the social systems that give their possessions value. In this sense, consumption becomes a meaning-making activity. Given that consumption does not take place in a vacuum, it is influenced by various factors such as social inequality, poverty and social class, which, in the case of South Africa, are also raced. In economically disadvantaged societies, consuming expensive commodities such as designer-label clothes signals access to resources (Mohamed 2011). In South Africa, this access to resources has its roots in the apartheid era, which conflated race and class and thus curtailed economic possibilities and upward social mobility for black people. Ratele (2011) argues that this structural violence led to the fetishisation of certain clothing brands for some young black men in townships. Quite often, the brands that are fetishised are seen in the media.

Both mass media and social media play a crucial role in disseminating information and disinformation that influence the process of identity enactment, behaviour, attitudes, values and perceptions (Allen 2007). Malinga and Ratele (2016: 101) note that the media contributes to constructing social and psychological meanings. Extending this view to print media, Narunsky-Laden (2008: 131) comments that 'consumer magazines for black South Africans function seminally as "cultural tools" that perform the task of cultural (re)ordering by codifying, disseminating, and legitimising specific urban middle-class repertoires for black South Africans'. Although we are in the digital era, where many rely more on electronic media than print media, this observation remains relevant since most print titles also have online editions.

Further, the media defines and legitimises certain masculine identities and ways of being and living over others (Malinga & Ratele 2016). Viljoen (2008, 2012) notes that magazines like *FHM, GQ, Destiny Men, Blink* and *Men's Health* tend to produce and reproduce hegemonic discourses of masculinity centred on middle-class consumerist ideals. This marginalises those who do not fit into these ideals and can give rise to 'resistant masculinities' (Malinga & Ratele 2016: 103). Though resistant masculinities differ across contexts, they are often characterised by 'rampant materialism, fatalistic attitudes, physical strength, and the acquisition of respect through violence' (Henry 2002: 116). The result of excessive exposure to the hegemonic masculine identities portrayed in the media is that they become naturalised. Living up to naturalised ideals of masculinity may often come at a cost, both financially and emotionally, especially for those men who live in impoverished conditions.

Kharnita Mohamed's (2011) study on the link between masculinity and consumption also focuses on the role of the media in the lives of young black men between the ages of 20 and 25 years at the University of the Western Cape. This historically disadvantaged institution previously catered to students predominantly from impoverished black communities (Willemse et al. 2018). Mohamed (2011: 105) found that 'clothing consumption was integral to the accrual of symbolic capital, the remaking of the social identities and the transformation of their masculinities'. To re-imagine and refashion their class identities and thus disarticulate race and class in post-apartheid South Africa, these young men drew extensively on hegemonic fantasies found in magazines such as *GQ* and *Men's Health* (Mohamed 2011: 105). Being a fluid, relational and multiple concept often influenced by power and class relations (Connell 1995), notions of hegemonic masculinity often overlap with and contradict each other (Morrell et al. 2012). In this sense, Mohamed (2011) notes that the young men in her study negotiated the upper-class masculinities from the magazines with black township masculinities to resignify their class aspirations strategically. The students in the study wore branded denim jeans, tracksuit pants, T-shirts, jackets and shoes. Their dress sense was geared towards the performance of their imagined masculinity.

Through their modes of dress, the young men sought to contest and refuse the identification with the perceived violent, lower-class black masculinities often associated with the Cape Flats (Du Toit 2014). The students used what Mohamed (2011) labels the performative possibilities of clothing, speech and other markers to locate them within the referential discourses that define middle-class masculinity. The motivation of these students was to move away from their habitual class dispositions (Mohamed 2011: 106). The upper-class masculinities represented in their magazines of choice suggested a current fashion sense. Mohamed notes that clothing enables self-representation, individual differentiation, and symbolic inclusion into a social identity. Using clothes to communicate class membership or at least a certain social identity conjures up notions of sartorial expression.

In Chapter 6, I discussed the aspect of aspiration in this BoP segment. Aspiration requires a reference point, and in Mohamed's study, the media become one. The aspirations of people in the BoP segment are often tied to what they see in the media. In the context of *ukukhothana*, the participants often refer to figures with whom they identify and with whom they have a parasocial relationship. This is a one-sided relationship in which a person extends emotional energy, interest and time to another person they usually see in the media, such as celebrities. That person is often unaware of their existence.

This becomes particularly interesting in the case of the *izikhothane*, who have been reported to have this type of relationship with media personalities and business people – most notably with 'Sushi King', Kenny Kunene. Kunene, cited as the celebrity with a parasocial relationship with *izikhothane*, hosted an *izikhothane* bash in 2012 as part of his 42nd birthday party celebration.[3] This speaks to the media's role in how people in the BoP segment – and particularly *izikhothane* – consume and fashion their ideals of masculinity. Vega, one of the members of The Good Fellas, uniquely captures the idea of the role of the media in inspiring consumption:

> Like this is something that would make you want to change your life because such things we only see in movies with the bosses walking around with it. So, you need to act likewise.

The media is perceived as a window to reality. Often, the media portrays images that inform some people's identities. In the quote above, Vega alludes to this fact when speaking about his observation of male actors in movies living the life he wants. The Good Fellas report how, through the media, they see how men are portrayed as important in establishing a household, and the presence of money is key in this.

Not only do they see gender roles portrayed in the media, but they also note how they are inspired to wear certain clothes that they see as trendy and fashionable.

The Good Fellas' aspirations are informed by masculinities portrayed on programmes such as *Isibaya* (a soap opera on DSTV) and *Material Culture*, which airs every Sunday on *Mzansi Magic*. This reality show features arguably the most popular *skhothane* crew in the country, called Material Culture. Since it depicts the lives of *izikhothane*, this show resonates with The Good Fellas, where they often obtain tips on, for example, how to be a good father. The pursuit of women also features prominently on the show, and The Good Fellas often speak about how this is similar to their way of doing things. They aspire to see their crew being as strong as *Material Culture* and often ask me to help them become an even more successful crew of *izikhothane*.

The masculine citizen

An element of aspirational masculinity I have not discussed until now is that of citizenship. This alludes to the desire to develop one's community while still aspiring for a better life for oneself. While the general public disapproves of *izikhothane*, The Good Fellas have demonstrated the desire to create a better community through initiating and participating in community development, such as the annual Miss Masakhane Beauty Pageant. The pageant was started by Siya, a former Good Fella, in 2008. Siya explains:

> ... We had a problem of high teenage pregnancy. If I remember correctly, Thembisa schools were in the top five schools with high teenage pregnancy in Gauteng. As an event organiser myself, I realised that the kind of recreational sports that we have in this township, such as soccer tournaments, being the Philly's Games and the Easter Games, mainly cater for boys, and girls do not participate.

The Good Fellas are responsible for marketing the beauty pageant and its entertainment aspect. They use the pageant's status and popularity in their community to draw audiences and participants.

Figure 8.5 *Audience inside the Sam Hlalele Hall at the 2018 Miss Masakhane Beauty Pageant*

Figure 8.6 *The Good Fellas come on stage to perform at the 2018 Miss Masakhane Beauty Pageant*

Source: Images supplied by author.

In 2018, Rabbi Letageng, a member of The Good Fellas, started the Rabbi Letageng Youth Foundation (RLYF), a community engagement that The Good Fellas are part of. According to the organisation's Facebook page, the aim of RLYF is to serve the needs of the community.

What they do is focus on addressing socioeconomic factors and educate them on the importance of living in a safe and healthy environment. The municipality of Ekurhuleni tries by all means necessary to make the community to be clean as possible, as youth they want to give back to the community.

During an interview, Rabbi said:

> As you can see that our location has a lot of dump and this poses a lot of health risks because of the pollution. I decided to start the Rabbi Letageng Youth Foundation (RLYF), which is an environmental communication organisation. We educate the youth about the importance of preventing pollution and ensuring that we live in a clean and healthy environment. RLYF is an initiative by the youth aimed at tackling socioeconomic issues involving the youth. We are more concerned about health though as all effects of behaviour affect health at the end of the day. Our aim is not to really change our youth doings, [but] rather [to] educate them about the effects of their behaviour on the environment, themselves, their families, and society as a whole. Responsibility is what we aim to instil in the youth.

Figure 8.7 *RLYF Facebook post*

The main reason why the occupants of the community contract a lot of contagious diseases ...the Rabbi Letageng youth foundation aims to alert people about the diseases at the disposal of the occupants of the community and also educate the occupants about the importance of living in a healthy environment
#❸
#RLYF
#4theYouth_byTheYouth

Source: Image supplied by author.

The RLYF is aimed at reducing pollution in Phomolong. The foundation also visits schools to which they give motivational talks and career guidance. The organisation depends on the support of the community and The Good Fellas. Rabbi mentions that the status and fame of The Good Fellas in the community make it easy for the organisation to garner support. Thus, whenever RLYF runs campaigns, he leverages this fame.

My journey with The Good Fellas has been very interesting as I saw them participating in *ukukhothana* through various stages of their lives. Like most *izikhothane*, The Good Fellas have gone through much growth to become who they are today. Initially the group members used to engage in conspicuous destruction in order to get respect from their peers and elevate their social status. However, as they grew older, they abandoned the destructive elements of the subculture. The Good Fellas note that being a *skhothane* for them is part of growing up and will end as they grow older. Beyond being part of growing up, *ukukhothana* enables them to participate in societal initiatives that benefit others in the community, such as the RLYF and Miss Masakhane Beauty Pageant.

I have realised that although *izikhothane* do not come from affluent backgrounds, their financial situations vary, and some are better off than others. Their families' financial situations have taught the members of this crew the importance of hustling for themselves and learning how to manage their financial resources. This is evident in how they skillfully husband their money through sacrifices to buy the things they want. *Ukukhothana* plays a significant role in the performance of masculine identities, enacted through conspicuous consumption. It became clear to me that the pursuit of masculinities in *ukukhothana* is influenced mainly by set standards of manhood in society, as opposed to something that they make up on their own.

I discovered that the notion of manhood among The Good Fellas is predicated on doing, as opposed to just being a man. One needs to do or have a number of things to be considered manly or masculine, according to the crew members. Firstly, The Good Fellas consider money as very important to be considered a man.

Money is an important enabling resource when engaging in conspicuous consumption or caring for one's family. They place a huge emphasis on working, or hustling as they call it, through a business of some kind in order to get money. To The Good Fellas, a male who depends on his parents to give him money is not considered a real man.

Secondly, dating multiple partners and having sex with them is crucial to The Good Fellas, to the point where they mock those who do not manage to have a one-night stand with a woman after a night of partying or after an event. As they put it, 'he is a person that does not understand *ama*rush hour'.

Thirdly, for these men, drinking alcohol serves an important homosocial bonding purpose. Homosocial relationships are not sexual but friendly and occur among people of the same gender. In this instance, homosocial bonding means that while drinking they are able to open up to each other, mock each other, and laugh together, among other things. Alcohol makes events and get-togethers fun and brings them closer together. The ability to buy certain brands of alcohol that are popular and considered 'cool' elevates their social status. As they note, some brands, such as Carling Black Label beer, are associated with a lower class and would diminish their social status.

Finally, expensive clothes play a crucial role, acting as social skins that hide their poverty in public. Expensive clothes make people take them seriously and generate the respect they desire.

The Good Fellas do not consume only to satisfy immediate needs. Their consumption is also predicated on the desire to become: the need to tap into a life and a standard of living they are not experiencing. It is in part conspicuous but mostly aspirational. Their engagement in conspicuous consumption serves a rehumanising role, as the dehumanising effects of poverty are deeply felt.

The Good Fellas' consumption behaviour is not random; it is carefully orchestrated. How alcohol, food and clothes are displayed, and the timing and planning of this exercise are all linked and aligned to achieving a specific goal – creating a desired identity. An attempt to explain this behaviour through conspicuous consumption theory seems inadequate. Originally, Veblen's theory of conspicuous consumption and the leisure class explained the behaviour of the wealthy as a way to distinguish themselves from those stationed below them in the socioeconomic strata. It also suggested that these consumers wanted to show their peers they were superior by putting their wealth in evidence.

The Good Fellas' reasons for engaging in conspicuous consumption and the results of this engagement differ from those of Veblen's leisure class. The opposite is true: The Good Fellas' consumption illuminates the contrast between their extravagance and impoverishment. The Good Fellas do not think they are rich when they engage in conspicuous consumption. And, when other people look at The Good Fellas, they do not consider them to be putting their wealth in evidence because everybody knows this wealth does not exist. However, their behaviour does elevate their social status among their peers, so it has elements of conspicuous consumption.

The notion of masculinity is very fluid and contextual. The pursuit of masculinity is largely the pursuit of attaining attributes that are considered to define manhood in a particular society. In most cases, these attributes enjoy a hegemonic status in their context. The Good Fellas perceive the hegemonic masculinity in their community as predicated on financial resources that give them access to various privileges, such as respect from their peers. Another attribute of this masculine identity is being involved in heterosexual relationships with multiple sexual partners.

The desire to fit into a particular social group or identity undoubtedly triggers specific behaviours associated with inhabiting that space, and so it is with masculinity. The desire to be received and perceived as men within a consumerist society that predominantly allows the markets to facilitate the meaning of manhood largely disadvantages those who cannot measure up. What remains is the aspiration to attain masculinity. At this point, one notices the rise of aspirational masculinities.

Notes

1 A type of dance that involves moving the hips side to side. Originally the term came from a language called Lingala, mainly spoken in the Democratic Republic of Congo.
2 Kgafe G and Msibi S (2012) A birthday fit for a Sushi King. *Sowetan Live*, 26 October. https://www.pressreader.com/south-africa/sowetan/20121025/281500748499958

9 Consumption and social change

At the height of the apartheid regime, South African music legend, the late Miriam Makeba released a song titled *Khawuleza* (an isiXhosa word that means 'hurry up'). The song is about children who would scream, 'Hurry up, Mama, look, the police are coming, don't let them catch you!' whenever they saw a *kwela* (police van) approaching to raid their homes for different items. One such item would be alcohol. In 1897 the sale of alcohol to black people was outlawed, making it illegal for black people to drink what was referred to as the 'white man's liquor' (Edwards 1988), which included spirits, fortified and natural wines, and beer produced commercially by the big breweries. Alcohol restrictions ranged from strict prohibition to moderate drinking freedom through beer halls and women's home brewing (regularly followed by home raids). This lasted until the 1960s, when the Liquor Act was amended.

One of the most salient characteristics of music is its ability to delineate the state of social affairs within a country at a given time. Makeba's hit, *Khawuleza*, uniquely captures consumption under the regime of oppression in South Africa, when consumption and race were conflated. The song suggests that consumption patterns were propelled and curtailed by the official racial category within which they belonged. As such, black consumption was legislatively determined. Any form of consumption that suggested deviation from the law invited punishment.

The conversation about consumption is complex and multilayered, even more so in the South African context, because here, it cannot take place without locating it within the history of colonialism and apartheid. Posel (2010) argues that in a country that for decades denied the black majority's claim to citizenship and restricted what they could consume, conspicuous consumption is more than a signal of wealth or status: it symbolises belonging and freedom from apartheid. This brings me to the argument that consumption can reflect social change.

At the heart of the quest for liberation in South Africa is the topic of social change. In this chapter, I want to locate this conversation within the country's consumption landscape and explore how it potentially offers a lens through which to read social change. Consumption patterns can help make sense of the repertoires of change and identify areas and forms of change, as well as the gaps for intervention. While the laws around racial segregation were stringent, they did make provisions for social mobility and racial reclassification based on consumption patterns. According to Debrorah Posel (2010: 166):

> A provision of the 1936 Representation of Natives Act allowed a male 'native' to petition the Minister of the Interior to be classified as 'non-native', on the grounds of being 'a person of repute', demonstrating 'intellectual or other attainments more characteristic of European or other non-natives than natives [and] conforming in regard to his standards and habits of life to the standards and habits of life of Europeans' (Union of South Africa 1936, section 41). While primarily an acknowledgement of appropriate levels of education, this clause named and consolidated the nexus between race and distinction: the option of being declared 'non-native' was clearly not intended for the ill-dressed or unmannered, or for those otherwise lacking in the social distinction afforded by appropriate material ownership and display.

Thus, racial mobility was possible as a function of consumption. From this logic, one can surmise that consumption may equally indicate social stratification, whether real, imagined, or aspired to. As such, consumption offers a unique window through which to analyse social change in post-apartheid South Africa.

On social change

Social change refers to societal transformations at a micro or macro level. The government often drives social change at the macro level through policy reform and implementation. At the micro level, change may result from individual or subgroup responses to environmental factors. Social change at the macro level is often dramatic, with profound consequences for societal transformation and evident effects on the historical trajectory of a society.

The South African political landscape presents a perfect example of dramatic social change. The institution of the apartheid regime followed the victory of the National Party in 1948. Apartheid – the implementation of what a chief architect of the regime, Hendrick Verwoerd, labelled a 'system of good neighbourliness' – presents governmental engineering of dramatic social change predicated on racial differentiation. Racial segregation meant that whiteness would reign over all other defined races with consequences for movement, habitation and consumption, among other things.

However, dramatic social change in the country dates back to colonialism and the Union of South Africa. For example, the Natives Land Act 27 of 1913 prohibited black people, whom it referred to as natives, from land ownership and acquisition. This Act brought about territorial segregation based on race, locating black people on the peripheries of white cities and towns and only allowing them to enter these areas as workers and servants (Ellapen 2007). Land ownership is essential for human survival and dignity, and being dispossessed of it is dehumanising. The location of black people on the peripheries of the white cities and their presence in cities only as workers or servants affected their consumption of clothes, which, in turn, distinctively identified them as workers. The clothes that black people had to wear as workers and servants cemented their lowly, dehumanised position in society. Some escaped through their imaginative, liberating dress style, which symbolised social mobility (Corrigall 2015: 146).

Following years of struggle, the first multiracial elections were held in 1994, resulting in a landslide defeat of the National Party, with the African National Congress emerging as the governing party. The inauguration of Nelson Mandela as the first black president of South Africa heralded the new dawn – again, a time for dramatic social change. The promise of a better life for all – the electioneering slogan of the ruling party – encapsulated a reimagined life in which education would be free, decent housing would be provided, better health care would be accessible, there would be jobs for everyone and a reinstatement of dignity and freedom: essentially it would be a process of rehumanising the black body that had suffered decades of unscrupulous domination under the white minority rule.

People tend to re-evaluate their prevailing circumstances in times of dramatic social change. They compare promised changes to their experienced realities. A good position is one where the promises and the lived experiences are in harmony. In instances where the two are in contradiction, attempts to reduce the dissonance will ensue. In South Africa after 1994, the promise of a better life for all seems to have remained just that for many previously disenfranchised South Africans (Barolsky, 2012). While significant economic and social reforms sought to bring about change in South Africans' lives, the sad reality is that the economic reforms have benefited only a few black people, with most continuing to wallow in abject poverty. What makes this worse is that the wealth of the few is conspicuously displayed for observation. This is not to suggest that conspicuity is always aimed at 'showing off' performatively to the poor, though there are many instances. There are many indicators of social change, and consumption is one of the most salient ones in the South African context.

Conspicuous consumption as a catalyst for social change

There exists a unique link between consumption and social change. I could even argue that social change is abstract, and consumption is what transports it into the physical world. Conspicuous consumption is often criticised for its apparent extravagance and wastefulness. However, among *izikhothane* it can also be viewed as a catalyst for social change: redefining success and aspirations, encouraging entrepreneurship, and highlighting inequality and socioeconomic issues.

Redefining success and aspirations

The practices of The Good Fellas challenge conventional definitions of success and aspiration, which often revolve around stable employment, education and long-term financial security. The Good Fellas, however, challenge these norms by not delaying their gratification, using consumption. The push to redefine notions of success and aspirations within *ukukhothana* is often done through the performance of ideals of masculinities and 'manhood' seemingly linked to the capacity to consume. Essentially, *izikhothane* perform the idea of success and demonstrate their aspirations. This redefinition forces a broader reflection on the accessibility and relevance of traditional success metrics for marginalised communities.

In the time I spent with The Good Fellas, it became clear that being a man is not a state of being but a state of doing. According to The Good Fellas, actions make one a man, and this came through in the narratives about work, females, family and aspirations. Discussions about manhood and masculinity were often premised on the words 'as a man', followed by things a man needs to do. The quotations below, taken from interviews I conducted with members of The Good Fellas, illustrate this observation:

> As a man, you need to push your hustle, *nje ngeTariyane* [work hard like an Italian]. This is what I always tell my guys: that you need to hustle *kumele uspine* [you have to work hard]. A poor man doesn't sleep; only white men should sleep because they have money. I often wake up and go to my uncle's workshop and work on two cars at least, and get some money then go to my friends and show them how much I made while they were busy sleeping. (Vega)

> Staying with my grandmother, as a man, I feel that it gives me the freedom I need because at this age, now and then, I need to sneak in a different girl home. Now imagine if I had to do that staying with my parents in a room inside the house. Or having to return home from a night of heavy partying at the crack of dawn. My mother would never allow that. (Sibusiso, aka Snamzo)

> You know, as a man, you should not let people take advantage of you and disrespect you, you should make people respect you … And obviously, as a man you need three things: clothes, alcohol, and girls! If you have this

combination, you are sorted. And I must say that, man, being a *s'khothane* has really groomed me. I have a lot of experience, man. I know more than what other guys my age know about sex. (Mthingo)

The Good Fellas' actions determine their manhood: dating more than one woman, being able to hustle for themselves, being able to command respect from people, drinking alcohol, and dressing well. Talking about manhood as being something that one does, wherein those who do not behave in the same way are considered less of a man, speaks to notions of hegemonic masculinity. While I have discussed this idea in Chapter 7, I wish to foreground it further here to explain how the idea of performativity is connected to the notion of social change.

In *Gender Trouble*, Judith Butler (1990) argues that gender is not something that one is but something that one does. According to Butler (1990: 33), 'Gender is the repeated stylization of the body, a set of repeated acts within a highly rigid regulatory frame that congeal over time to produce the appearance of substance, of a natural sort of being'. The repeated and replicated ways of being a man in a particular community gain dominance over other less popular ones and are imbued with hegemonic status. In this sense, the notion of being a man is based on dominant societal ideals of manhood. Living up to these ideals makes a man an object of the respect that comes with inhabiting the space of hegemonic masculinity.

There are elements of hyper-masculinity that generally involve the exaggeration of the traits that define manhood. This was particularly evident among The Good Fellas when they were still young *izikhothane*. As they admitted during our individual interviews, this cost them a lot in terms of their education:

> I didn't complete my matric, man. I just decided to do my NCV [National Certificate Vocational qualification, equivalent to Grades 10, 11 and 12 of the National Senior Certificate and offered by Further Education and Training Colleges in South Africa] because I was expelled from school. They gave me a red card. The problem is that I used to get into a lot of fights, man, and eventually, in 2016, at the

age of 17, they got tired of me [and] kicked me out ... You know as a man you should not let people take advantage of you and disrespect you – you should make people respect you. So that was my downfall. (Mthingo)

I am currently doing Grade 11. In my life, I have failed twice (Grade 7 firstly, then again in high school). In high school, I failed because I wasn't focused on my studies. I was busy playing as a s'khothane. (Vega)

I am currently doing Grade 10 at the age of 18. The reason for this [is] because I have failed and repeated grades a number of times. This was mainly due to my focus on being izikhothane, which to be honest did distract me. (Manqoba)

I am currently doing Grade 11. Ideally, I should have my matric already, but I dropped out of my previous school. The school that I went to was a private school in Ivory Park for black people and the school fees were R 900 monthly – eish, you know, man, black people love money. It became too expensive for my mother since I wasn't doing well, so we agreed that I should go to another school, a cheaper one. I failed because I was very playful, man, and I dance a lot. Being a s'khothane contributed greatly to this. But now I am currently at a night school trying to complete my studies there. (Sihle, aka Bob)

The quotations above demonstrate how The Good Fellas have sought to exert their manhood through ways that have compromised their education, such as violent behaviour and a lack of focus on schooling. This aligns with other research about adolescent youths pursuing masculine identities, thereby compromising their academic performance (see Mchunu 2016; Mkhwanazi 2011). In the quote above, Bob mentions finances as one reason for dropping out of school. He does concede that his lack of focus at school, which resulted in him repeating grades, made it expensive for his mother because it meant that she had to pay for the extra years at school. His mother's continued expenditure on education highlights the importance she placed on attempting to give him a chance at a life that she herself never lived. Most members of The Good Fellas have repeated at least one grade because of their pursuit of a masculine identity, which took their attention from their schoolwork.

As bad as it was, it seems that growth over the years has helped the group get back on to 'the right path', as noted by Sibusiso, aka Mokongoana, who is currently doing his second year of Public Relations at Rosebank College:

> It just so happened that when I moved to Clayville and went to tertiary, I started drifting away from the group. Not because I wanted that to happen, but because of my commitment to education I no longer had enough time to hang with the guys. But somehow, my drifting away because of education inspired my friends to study as well, because they saw the importance of education because some of them had even dropped out of school. I remember at one-point Vega even wanted to drop out because he had failed. But I had a talk with him, and he decided not to drop out. As we speak, now he is the president of the SRC at his school. Mthingo as well is now studying. We also had ideas about growing the group, even making money from it. This is where the idea [came] of making T-shirts like the one you have with the name of The Good Fellas printed on it. I want us to push big events, man. I know that there are guys I can trust in the group when it comes to doing such things; guys like Vega and Rabbi to push events. But for now, we will go with what we have. (Sibusiso, aka Mokongoana)

The growth of the members of this subculture became apparent during our conversations. It became clear to me that being a *s'khothane* was, more than anything, part of growing up in an environment where there are limited options in terms of life choices and information about what one could do recreationally other than play soccer.

According to the *izikhothane*, they still encounter a shortage of people to look up to. This results in them not being sufficiently inspired by those immediately accessible to them. For example, during our interview, Vega said:

> But I have since learned my lesson and I am now pushing very hard. Even if you were to see my marks now you would realise that I am not playing games. My problem, though, when I think about post-matric, is that I have no one who is inspiring me or motivating me through advice as to how to go about furthering my studies because, man, our township is bit low on such people.

The issue raised about people to look up to is evident in the current 'hustles' and the life trajectories of The Good Fellas, as they tend to do similar work to what their parents, guardians other close members of the community do. For example, Vega, whose uncle has a panel beater's workshop, hustles by working there. Snamzo, whose mother has a car registration printing business in which they deal a lot with taxis, has found himself in the taxi-driving business. Snamzo explains:

> You know, bro, as a man I have to push my own hustle. I can't at this age expect my parents to give me money to buy Fabiani clothes, man, I need to earn my keep. I drive a staff bus. I pick up late staff from the airport in the evening. I start work at 19:00, finish at 12 am. I got into this taxi-driving business because it is what I see people in my area doing, so at least they become my contacts that enable me to get into the industry.

What I have also found particularly interesting is the existence of three categories of people in this group. There are those who possess what Bourdieu (1986) refers to as cultural capital, those who do not possess it, and those who attain the benefits of cultural capital without having it.

In the first category are those whose parents or guardians work as administrators, which, in this context, is considered decent and superior because it is an office job in which one does paperwork and uses a computer. This occupation is also more affluent than other blue-collar occupations. Administrators are considered more educated because they have either matric or at least one post-matric qualification.

The crew members with parents in this category somehow tend to push further in education. They may have failed but have never dropped out. They seem to envision getting white-collar jobs like their parents or guardians. This exemplifies Bourdieu's (1986) theory of cultural reproduction, which posits that children from middle-class families are advantaged in attaining education and subsequent credentials due to their possession of cultural capital (Sullivan, 2001: 1). The concept of middle class is complex, with unhinged parameters. Keeley (2015) notes that the middle class is 'somewhere above poor but below rich, but where?' Speaking about these crew members as belonging to middle-class households is problematic because they come from families with some elements of being middle class but with meagre incomes. During an interview that I had with Rabbi, he said:

> My mother works for a logistics company but I am not sure what it is that she does, but I know she is always on her laptop. By the way, she recently graduated with a diploma in something. She inspires me. That is why I also want to make sure that I finish my studies and get a good office job. I can't stand doing hard labour.

This quotation speaks to Rabbi's aspirations. Other members of the group who possessed cultural capital said similar things.

In contrast, there are those who do not possess cultural capital and are, in this sense, disadvantaged. For example, Mpho (Sekatana), whose mother is a general worker at the pigment-manufacturing factory and has no matric, has failed to attain his matric and is currently working at Spar as a general worker.

In the third category, we have crew members like Vega, whose parents, or his guardians when he became orphaned, do not have cultural capital. Yet, he is pursuing education with an understanding that it is a possible way out of his impoverished condition. This brings to the fore the idea of how the surroundings of an individual influence the type of direction that they may want to take. Essentially, this means one's surroundings may offer a good reference point for determining what one wants or does not want to become.

The concept of three categories should not be misunderstood as implying that the group members follow only their parents' or guardians' trajectories but rather that their surroundings influence their drive for a better life. They are strong individuals with agency. For many participants, *ukukhothana* is a way to assert their identity and reclaim dignity in a society where they may still feel marginalised. They make a statement about their socioeconomic agency by showcasing their ability to purchase and destroy expensive goods.

Economic implications and entrepreneurship

The subculture of *ukukhothana* indirectly encourages entrepreneurial thinking. The need to finance a conspicuous lifestyle often leads participants to seek innovative ways to generate income. Some crew members have leveraged their notoriety and style to create business opportunities. This entrepreneurial spirit, albeit driven by a desire for conspicuous consumption, can contribute to local economic development and inspire others to pursue similar paths.

Often when people try to make sense of the behaviour of *izikhothane*, the question of affordability arises. Well, the answer to that is 'hustle'. They have different ways of hustling. The word 'hustle' relates to doing whatever you must, to get what you want. They explained to me that to hustle does not involve doing illegal things. The saying *Itariyane kwamele lispine* ('an Italian must work hard') refers to a person who wears expensive Italian brands but must first *spine* – work hard. For example, Vega works at a panel-beating workshop, a skill he learned from his uncle. Manqoba owns a car wash, which he says his father started for him, and he then took over.

When some members do not work or have businesses, their parents always step in to assist them, not necessarily to be izikhothane but to show their children love by providing them with things they never had when growing up and having them dress up well. The lengths these young men go to look great speak volumes about consumption. Lury (1996) suggests that consumption patterns should be read as communication messages with consequence and social meaning (see also Douglas & Isherwood 1979: 11; McCracken 1990). The attainment of the displayed lifestyle of leisure is preceded by hard work. This attainment is considered victorious because they constantly run the risk of losing.

For The Good Fellas, earning a living forms a big part of a dignified life. Not only does it enable them to afford the things they need, but it also gives them a sense of responsibility. The ability to work for their money is a source of great pride among the members of the crew, who mock those who depend on their parents for money and call them 'spoilt brats'. Since The Good Fellas are mostly students, their hustles often occur outside school hours. Their jobs are in the informal sector and mainly involve menial labour. Vega joked during one of our conversations, saying *indoda kwamele ijuluke*, meaning that a man must sweat at work. The sweat gives them the sense of pride with which they engage in the conspicuous consumption that the subculture is known for.

Figure 9.1 *Manqoba at his car wash in Phomolong*

Source: Image supplied by author.

Apart from the car wash, some members have businesses selling snacks and sweets at school. Though selling things that students need at school is done in the open, there are some things that are sold in secret, as the school would not approve of selling them on their grounds. Katlego, nicknamed Skopo, told me during one of our conversations at the taxi rank, where we often met for one-on-one interviews, that he also sold cigarettes. He explained to me that the cigarette business was very lucrative at school as most boys were experimenting with smoking, and therefore it made him a lot of money. However, as smoking was prohibited at school, he always resorted to hiding the cigarettes. When I asked about the age of his customers he simply chuckled and said, 'I give people what they want'.

The ability to earn one's money put The Good Fellas at ease in the face of criticism of their conspicuous consumption. They explained that wasting something you worked hard for was better than wasting someone else's efforts, so they were not bothered by what people said.

Shortfalls of consumption as a catalyst for social change

While consumption plays a big role in catalysing social change, it comes with many pitfalls that may, if not resolved, hinder the desired social change. These pitfalls include superficiality, misaligned incentives, fragmentation of efforts, and distraction from collective action.

Superficial and symbolic change

The subculture of *ukukhothana* is fundamentally about visible displays of wealth and social status. Participants spend a lot of money on branded clothing, shoes and accessories, which are then destroyed in public spectacles. This practice serves as a symbolic assertion of socioeconomic agency, yet it does little to address the structural issues underlying economic disparities in South Africa. The impact of such displays is limited to the immediate social recognition within the group, offering an ephemeral sense of empowerment rather than enduring change. Like many consumer trends, the influence of *ukukhothana* is transient, and its ability to inspire long-term social transformation is questionable.

Misalignment of incentives

Izikhothane also illustrates the misalignment of incentives in a consumer-driven social movement. The commercial interests of brands and companies capitalise on people's desires, such as those of *izikhothane*, and promote luxury goods without contributing to community socioeconomic advancement. This commercialisation prioritises profit over genuine social responsibility. Consequently, the destructive displays of *izikhothane* can be seen as a form of conspicuous consumption that benefits companies more than the individuals or communities involved.

Fragmentation of efforts

The fragmentation of efforts is evident in the subculture of *ukukhothana*. The focus on individual acts of conspicuous consumption distracts from more unified, strategic approaches to addressing systemic issues. Rather than concentrating on collective action to tackle economic inequality, efforts are dispersed among individual displays of wealth. This fragmentation dilutes the potential for significant, coordinated progress towards social justice and economic reform.

Distraction from collective action

Perhaps most critically, *ukukhothana* distracts from collective action and policy advocacy, essential for achieving systemic change. The subculture's emphasis on individual consumption diverts attention from grassroots organising, political activism, and institutional reform. These broader efforts are crucial for addressing deep-seated socioeconomic issues in South Africa. By focusing on immediate, visible displays of wealth, izikhothane may overlook the importance of sustained, collective efforts to create lasting social transformation.

Note

1   See also Blignaut C & Sithole S (2014) The twisted tale of alcohol and apartheid. *News24*. Accessed 22 April 2016, http://www.news24.com/Archives/City-Press/Twisted-tale-of-alcohol-andapartheid-20150429

10 Conclusion: Is manhood for sale?

This book sets out to investigate the relationship between consumption, masculinities and communication. The aim is to understand the role of conspicuous consumption in the expression of masculinities among the participants in *ukukhothana*. To that end, I have written an ethnographic account of The Good Fellas, who are a crew of *izikhothane* from Thembisa.

It is important to note that the community of Thembisa is not homogeneous, and notions of masculinity are not the same for everyone in the township. The traits of masculinity that I grapple with in this book are pertinent to the context of The Good Fellas. Their burning desire manifests itself through aspirational consumption.

Locating a single grand theory that could help me make sense of *ukukhothana* by considering conspicuous consumption and the communication of masculinities was a difficult task. As a result, I opted to rely on various theoretical lenses, each of which has enabled me to explain specific aspects of the subculture. I first turned my attention to work done on subcultures, mainly to provide an angle from which *ukukhothana* should be understood as a subculture in the contemporary era. Thus, I have briefly looked at the development of subcultural theory and then discussed post-subculture theory, recognising *izikhothane* as a unique subculture.

My discussion of *ukukhothana* as a subculture deviates from the subculture theory produced by the Birmingham Centre for Contemporary Cultural Studies and from Dick Hebdige's (1979) notion of resistance. Instead, I position my discussion within the framework of discursive resistance, in the sense of the subculture discursively revealing a deep desire for that which one might appear not to want. For example, the destruction of clothes is not because *izikhothane* do not desire these clothes, nor is it a demonstration of having them in abundance. Further, it is not a form of resisting expensive clothes. Rather, the destruction seeks to resist and challenge associations with poverty and the perceived lack of options that come with this association. It demonstrates desiring a 'way of not being like that', as Death (2016) puts it.

Moreover, the destruction demonstrates a desire to attain a high social status amongst one's peers. As such, destruction is not carried out as a form of resistance or protest against the dominant values of society, which are largely encapsulated in conspicuous consumption. The destruction is an attempt to not only live up to perceived societal values that place a high premium on consumption and the meanings that may be gleaned from it but also to transcend them in an exaggerated manner.

Having established the context from which I discuss The Good Fellas as a subculture, I move on to the concept of conspicuous consumption. This discussion begins with the work of Thorstein Veblen (1899), who coined the concept in his seminal book *The Theory of the Leisure Class*. Veblen (1899/2003) thought that the 'leisure class' particularly engaged in wasteful conspicuous consumption because, in their pursuit of honour, they 'put their wealth in evidence' through spectacular parties and expensive clothes. While showing off to their peers, the excessive consumption of the leisure class also served to underline clear class differences, distancing its members from lower-class productive labour and parsimony.

Neither Veblen nor social commentators in South Africa could have foreseen the rise of *ukukhothana*. Although the diamond field dandies and *oswenka* offer historical examples of poor black men who spent inordinate amounts of money on clothes (and, in the latter case competed for sartorial honour), commentators have been puzzled by *ukukhothana's* 'destructive wastefulness'. From Veblen's perspective, one could also see their performances as failed attempts to gain honour, especially since the young men fool no one into thinking that they are, contrary to general knowledge, rich or fall into the leisure class.

In this book, I have tried to dispel some of the perceptions that frame *ukukhothana* in a solely negative light by looking at the ways in which *izikhothane* view their competition and give meaning to their consumption. I argue that while *izikhothane* want to escape their poverty, they do not see the *ukukhothana* lifestyle as a (deluded) way out of poverty. Instead, while wildly aspirant, most *izikhothane* see their participation in this youth culture as a fun part of their youth and a means to generate social status among their peers.

Behind the scenes, crews such as The Good Fellas work hard to buy expensive clothes and make many sacrifices to participate in this lifestyle. The rewards include popularity and respect for being stylish 'hustlers', especially when their hard-earned booty catches fire Mnisi (2019: 179). Unlike Veblen's lower-class imitators, these young men are deeply creative in assembling outfits and mixing branded clothes with cheaper ones. Further, unlike Veblen's (1899) individualists, their consumption also points to other groups of young men who use their consumption to create a group identity and cohesion. Thus, there is much more to the *izikhothane's* performances than simply a misplaced hankering for 'honour' or fame.

The communicative role of consumption is indisputably crucial and complex, especially regarding the expression of identity. The Good Fellas use consumption to perform and express aspirational masculinities. For the crew members, being a man is about doing certain things; failing disqualifies one. For The Good Fellas, a man needs to have money as it enables him to take care of himself and provide for his family. The idea of having money is tightly linked to the ability to hustle for money. Men who obtain money from their parents are considered less manly and even spoilt.

The nature of the hustles in which The Good Fellas involve themselves seems strongly correlated with their parents' or guardians' means of earning a living. Though this is the case, it became evident from my interactions with the crew members that they often want more for themselves and desire to do better than their parents, as they have bigger aspirations. Having grown older, they have now realised the importance of education. Their first priority is getting through school as the initial step towards living a better life. In their interviews with me, they mentioned how they used up valuable time in their early days of participating in *ukukhothana*. Unfortunately, this forced them to repeat at least one grade, with some losing up to three years.

CONCLUSION: IS MANHOOD FOR SALE?

Along with aspirational consumption, The Good Fellas highly prize sexual conquest. They often refer to the pursuit of girls for one-night stands at the end of a night out as the 'rush hour'. A clear understanding of rush hour is that if one plays one's cards right, which means impressing the women with alcohol, dance, clothes and overall 'coolness', one can 'catch' the woman whom one had eyed throughout the night. The Good Fellas explain that this is crucial because one's manhood is in part tested through one's ability to have sexual intercourse with women – and not just with one but multiple partners. The more women one sleeps with, the more respected one is as 'a man'. It is important to remember that their actions are often influenced by what they see as 'the way of doing things' in their community. Patriarchal and sexist norms of judging manhood and objectifying women significantly influence The Good Fellas' actions.

Although The Good Fellas summarise the requirements of being considered masculine as attaining girls, expensive clothes, charm and alcohol, money is central. Once one has access to money, especially if one has worked hard, one can buy clothes and alcohol, entertain women, and perhaps even care for one's family. The notion of masculinity in this context thus centres around money. It raises the question of whether The Good Fellas conceive manhood as something that could be bought. Following this logic, manhood is not a state of being but rather a state of doing. A coherent set of activities ultimately determines whether one is worthy of being called a man.

In post-apartheid South Africa, these ideals of masculinity are influenced by the rampant consumerism evident in the country as well as on various media platforms. In addition, there is a clear understanding that attaining this form of masculine identity is predicated on hard work, followed by parades of elegance and the subsequent elevation of social status.

However, this singular notion of masculinity that seems to be enjoying a hegemonic status in the context of The Good Fellas needs to be further interrogated and problematised. There is value derived from these qualities and benefits to this type of identity, which is not just about wasteful conspicuous consumption. Some benefits can include learning to take responsibility at an early age for one's needs, understanding the importance of earning a living and playing a role in society by seeking to develop others and make a difference in the lives of other young people.

When we analyse and discuss *ukukhothana*, we ought to consider the multiplicity of masculinities it embodies, the very idea it displays that there is more than one way of being a man. Future researchers could delve into studies that seek to shed light on masculinities in the township that are not predicated on heteropatriarchal notions of manhood. Such research could also help us understand the disempowering nature of patriarchy, particularly on township youths.

The naturalisation of what it means to be a man also needs to be interrogated. The Good Fellas demonstrate a relentless pursuit of the hegemonic traits that define manhood as if they were the only option, which potentially speaks of the alternatives that are in front of them. This is to the detriment of some of their future goals. The key is to understand that there are many ways of being a man, and if the option you choose costs you more than it should, then it is probably not the best option to choose.

In conclusion, in the context of the subculture of *ukukhothana*, consumption operates as a communication vehicle through which the expression and performance of post-apartheid youth masculinities occur, which encapsulate ideals of aspiration. It is evident that the significant attributes of hegemonic masculinity, as they occur in this subculture, are linked mainly to the ability to consume exuberantly. Consumption capacity is associated with access to financial resources. The association between financial resources and consumption is then interpreted as masculine. However, since access to financial resources is, in reality, largely meagre and superficial, it makes sense to define this model of conspicuous consumption as aspirational and perhaps also to argue that the perceived identity of masculinity that emerges from this performance may be viewed as aspirational consumption.

Bibliography

Alland A (2002) *Race in mind: Race, IQ and other racisms*. New York: Palgrave Macmillan

Allen DG (2007) Recruitment communication media: Impact on pre-hire outcomes. *Personnel Psychology*, 57(1): 143–171

Al-Shawaf L & Lewis DMG (2017) *The handicap principle*. Accessed 20 March 2018, https://www.researchgate.net/publication/320660907_The_Handicap_Principle

Arronson T & Johansson-Stenman O (2012) *Keeping up with the Joneses, the Smiths and the Tanakas: On international tax coordination and social comparisons*. Accessed 13 May 2018, https://econpapers.repec.org/paper/hhsgunwpe/0621.htm

Bakhtin M (1984) *Rabelais and his world* (trans. H Iswolsky). Bloomington: Indiana University Press

Banerjee AV & Duflo E (2007) The economic lives of the poor. *Journal of Economic Perspectives*, 21(1): 141–167

Barolsky V (2012) 'A better life for all', social cohesion and the governance of life in post-apartheid South Africa. *Social Dynamics*, 38(1): 1–20

Bar-Tal D (2000) From intractable conflict through conflict resolution to reconciliation: Psychological analysis. *Political Psychology*, 21(2)

Baruch S & Kannai Y (2001) Inferior goods, Giffen goods, and Shochu. In G Debreu, W Neuefeind & W Trockel (eds) *Economics essays*. Switzerland: Springer

Baudrillard J (1998) *The consumer society: Myths and structures*. London: Sage

Baudrillard J (2005) *The system of objects*. London: Verso

Benedict R (1934) *Patterns of culture*. Boston and New York: The Riverside Press

Bennett A (1999) Subcultures or neo-tribes? Rethinking the relationship between youth, styles and musical taste. *Sociology* 33(3): 599–617

Benvenuto S (2000) Review of Georg Simmel's fashion. *Journal of Artificial Societies and Social Simulation*, 3(2): 133–143

Botz-Bornstein T (1995) Rule-following in dandyism: 'Style' as an overcoming of 'rule' and 'structure'. *Modern Humanities Research Association*, 90(2): 285–295

Bourdieu P (1984) *Distinction: A social critique of the judgement of taste.* London: Routledge & Kegan Paul

Bourdieu P (1986) The forms of capital. In JE Richardson (Ed.) *Handbook of Theory of Research for the Sociology of Education* (trans. R Nice). Westport: Greenword Press

Brdar I, Rijavec M & Dubravka M (2009) Life goals and well-being: Are extrinsic aspirations always detrimental to well-being? *Psychological Topics*, 18(2): 317–334

Burger R, Louw M, de Oliveira-Pegado BB & van der Berg S (2015) Understanding consumption patterns of the established and emerging South African black middle class. *Development Southern Africa*, 32(1): 41–56

Butler J (1990) *Gender trouble: Feminism and the subversion of identity.* London and New York: Routledge

Butler J (2011) *Bodies that matter: On the discursive limits of 'sex'.* London and New York: Routledge

Campbell C (1995) Conspicuous confusion? A critique of Veblen's theory of conspicuous consumption. *Sociological Theory*, 13(1): 37–47

Charles KK, Hurst E & Roussanov N (2009) Conspicuous consumption and race. *The Quarterly Journal of Economics*, 124(2): 425–467

Charoenrook A & Thakor A (2008) *Theory of conspicuous consumption.* Accessed 06 September 2012, https://www.academia.edu/20577981/A_Theory_of_Conspicuous_Consumption

Chase B, Legoete T & van Wamelen A (2010) *A seismic shift in South Africa's consumer landscape.* Accessed 10 September 2019, https://www.mckinsey.com/industries/consumer-packaged-goods/our-insights/a-seismic-shift-in-south-africas-consumer-landscape

Cheng KC (2008) Demystifying skin color and 'race'. In RE Hall (ed.) *Racism in the 21st century: An empirical analysis of skin color.* New York: Springer

Chipp K, Kapelianis D & Mkhwanazi P (2016) *Ukukhothana*: The curious case of conspicuous consumption and destruction in an emerging economy. In K Plangger (ed.) *Thriving in a new world economy. Developments in marketing science: Proceedings of the Academy of Marketing Science.* New York: Springer

Chisholm B (2018) *A-maize-ing: African food to sample in southern Africa.* Accessed 9 March 2019, https://www.africanbudgetsafaris.com/blog/a-maize-ing-grace-africas-delicious-food/

Christen M & Morgan RM (2005) Keeping up with the Joneses: Analysing the effect of income inequality on consumer borrowing. *Quantitative Marketing and Economics,* 3(2): 145–173

Cikszentmihalyi M & Rochberg-Halton E (1981) *The meaning of things: Domestic symbols and the self.* Cambridge: Cambridge University Press

CioIndex (2021) *Bottom of the Pyramid (BOP).* Accessed 1 April 2019, https://cio-wiki.org/wiki/Bottom_of_the_Pyramid_%28BOP%29

Connell RW (1995) *Masculinities.* Cambridge: Polity Press

Cope W & Kalantzis M (eds) (2015) *A pedagogy of multiliteracies: Learning by design.* London: Palgrave Macmillan

Corrigall M (2015) Sartorial excess in Mary Sibande's 'Sophie'. *Critical Arts,* 29(2): 146–164

Currod-Halkett E (2017) *The sum of small things: A theory of the aspirational class.* Princeton: Princeton University Press

Darwin C (1859) *On the origin of species by means of natural selection, or the preservation of favoured races in the struggle for life.* London: John Murray

De Beauvoir S (1974) *The second sex,* trans. H. M. Parshley. New York: Vintage

De Fraja (2009) The origin of utility: Sexual selection and conspicuous consumption. *Journal of Economic Behavior and Organization,* 72: 51–69

Death C (2010) Counter-conduct: A Foucauldian analytics of protest. *Social Movement Studies,* 9(3): 235–251

Death C (2016) Counter-conducts as a method of resistance: Ways of 'not being like that' in South Africa. *Global Society* 30(2): 201–217

Dinu G, Tanase AC, Dinu L & Tanase FD (2010) The new techniques for handling consumer behaviour. Paper presented at the International DAAAAM Symposium, Australia

Dinwoodie-Irving D (2010) *African cookboy.* Johannesburg: Jacana Press

Dittmar H (2008) *Consumer culture, identity and well-being: The search for the 'good life' and the 'body perfect'.* Canada and the United States of America: Psychology Press

Djellal F & Gallouj F (2014) *The laws of imitation and invention: Gabriel Tarde and the evolutionary economics of innovation*. Accessed 1 April 2019 https://halshs.archives-ouvertes.fr/halshs-00960607/document

Doi J, Iwasa K & Shimomura K (2009) Giffen behavior independent of wealth level. *Economic Theory*, 42(2): 247–267

Dolfsma W (2000) Life and times of Veblen effect. *History of Economic Ideas*, 8(3): 61–82

Dornbusch R (1985) *Purchasing power parity*. NBER Working Paper Series, Working Paper No. 1591. Accessed 1 April 2019, https://www.nber.org/papers/w1591.pdf

Douglas M & Isherwood B (1979) *The world of goods*. London: Allen Lane

Dreze X & Nunes JC (2009) Feeling superior: The impact of loyalty program structure on consumers' perception of status. *Journal of Consumer Research*, 35(6): 890–905

Du Plooy-Cilliers F & Louw M (2015) *Let's talk interpersonal communication* (4th ed.) South Africa: Pearson Education

Du Toit M (2014) Contextual factors and the experience of unemployment: A review of qualitative studies. *South African Journal of Economic and Management Sciences*, 21(1): 17–35

Dubow S (2014) *Apartheid: 1948–1994*. Oxford: Oxford University Press

During S (2005) *Cultural studies: A critical introduction*. New York: Routledge

Edwards I (1988) Shebeen queens: Illicit liquor and the social structure of drinking dens in Cato Manor. *Agenda*, 3: 75–97

Ellapen JA (2007) The cinematic township: Cinematic representations of the 'township space' and who can claim the rights to representation in post-apartheid South African cinema. *Journal of African Cultural Studies*, 19(1): 113–137

Firat AF & Venkatesh A (1995) Liberatory postmodernism and the reenchantment of consumption. *Journal of Consumer Research*, 22: 239–267

Fleminger D (2007) Swanky swenkas: Dressing sharp regardless of cost. *Vice*. Accessed 23 March 2017, http://www.vice.com/read/swank-b14n5

Fosnacht KJ (2013) Selectivity and the college experience: How undermatching shapes the college experience among high-achieving students. Presented at the American Educational Research Association Annual Meeting, Chicago, IL

Friedman J (1994) *Consumption and identity*. Reading: Harwood Academic Publishers

Frisch MB (1998) Quality of life therapy and assessment in health care. *Clinical Psychology: Science and Practice*, 5(1): 19–40

Frost S (2018) What is a player in dating? *Our Everyday Life*. Accessed 22 September 2019, https://oureverydaylife.com/player-dating-5137140.html

Gelder K & Thornton S (eds) (1997) *The subculture reader*. New York: Routledge

Ger G & Belk RW (1996) Cross-cultural differences in materialism. *The Journal of Economic Psychology*, 17: 55–77

Godelnik R (2012) 7 things you need to know about aspirational consumers. *Triple Pundit*. Accessed 29 April 2015, http://www.triplepundit.com/2012/12/aspirational-consumers/

Griskevicius V, Tybur J, Sundie J, Cialdini R, Miller G et al. (2007) Blatant benevolence & conspicuous consumption: When romantic motives elicit strategic costly signals. *Journal of Personality and Social Psychology*, 93: 85–102

Gumede W (2011) Tackling corruption. *Focus: Journal of the Helen Suzman Foundation*, 60: 15–23

Gupta S & Srivastav P (2016) An exploratory investigation of aspirational consumption at the bottom of the pyramid. *Journal of International Consumer Marketing*, 28(1): 2–15

Hamilton K & Catterall M (2006) Consuming love in poor families: Children's influence on consumption decisions. *Journal of Marketing Management*, 22(9-10): 1031–1052

Harris M (1974) *Cows, pigs, wars and witches: The riddles of culture*. New York: Random House

Hebdige D (1979) *Subculture: The meaning of style*. London: Routledge

Henry M (2002) He is a 'bad mother': Shaft and contemporary black masculinity. *Journal of Popular Film and Television*, 30(2): 114–119

Hill RP & Gaines J (2007) The consumer culture of poverty: Behavioural research findings and their implications in an ethnographic context. *Journal of American Culture*, 30(1): 81–95

Howell S & Vincent L (2014) 'Licking the snake' – the *I'khothane* and contemporary township youth identities in South Africa. *South African Review of Sociology*, 45(2): 60–77

Howie SJ, Combrinck C, Roux K, Tshele M, Mokoena GM & Palane N (2017) *PIRLS literacy 2016 progress in international reading literacy study: South African children's reading literacy achievement*. Pretoria: Centre for Evaluation and Assessment

Inggs A (2017) The suit is mine: Skhothane and the aesthetic of the African modern. *Critical Arts*, 31(3): 90–105

Iqani M (2015) Agency and affordability: Being black and 'middle class' in South Africa in 1989. *Critical Arts*, 29(2): 126–145

Jensen SQ (2006) Rethinking Subcultural Capital. *Young: Nordic Journal of You*, 14(3): 257–276

Jensen SQ (2011) Othering, identity formation and agency. *Qualitative Studies*, 2 (2): 63–78

Jones M (2013) Conspicuous destruction, aspiration and motion in the South African township. *Safundi*, 14(2): 209–224

Kasser T & Ryan RM (1996) Further examining the American dream: Differential correlates of intrinsic and extrinsic goals. *Journal of Personality and Social Psychology*, 22(3): 280–287

Kaus W (2010) *Conspicuous consumption and race: Evidence from South Africa*. Papers on Economics and Evolution No. 1003, Max Planck Institute of Economics. Accessed 20 February 2020, https://www.econstor.eu/dspace/bitstream/10419/32637/1/622802046.pdf

Keeley B (2015) *Income inequality: The gap between rich and poor*. Paris: OECD Insights

Kenton W (2019) *Inferior good*. Accessed 15 September 2019, https://www.investopedia.com/terms/i/inferior-good.asp

Kernani A (2007) Romanticizing the Poor Harms the Poor. *Metamorphosis: A Journal of Management Research*, 6(2): 151–162

Kleine RE III, Kleine SS & Kernan JB (1993) Mundane consumption and the self: A social-identity perspective. *Journal of Consumer Psychology*, 2(3): 209–235

Kohli M (1986) The institutionalization of the life course: Looking back to look ahead. *Research in Human Development*, 4(3): 253–271

Kolk A, Rivera-Santos M & Rufin C (2013) Reviewing a decade of research on the 'base/bottom of the pyramid' (BOP) concept. *Business & Society* pre-print: 1–40

Kotler P & Armstrong G (2015) *Marketing principles: Global and South African perspectives*. Cape Town: Pearson

Kugan J (2019) *Law of supply and demand*. Accessed 9 March 2019, https://www.investopedia.com/terms/l/law-of-supply-demand.asp

Lafrance R & Schembri L (2002) *Purchasing-power parity: Definition, measurement, and interpretation*. Bank of Canada, International Department. Accessed 1 April 2019, https://www.bankofcanada.ca/wp-content/uploads/2010/06/lafrance_e.pdf

Lamont M & Molnar V (2001) How Blacks use consumption to shape their identity: Evidence from marketing specialists. *Journal of Consumer Culture*, 1(1): 31–45

Langa M & Eagle G (2008) The intractability of militarised masculinity: A case study of former self-defence unit members in the Kathlorus area, South Africa. *South African Journal of Psychology*, 38(1): 152–175

Langa M (2012) Becoming a man: Exploring multiple voices of masculinity amongst a group of young adolescent boys in Alexandra Township, South Africa. PhD dissertation. Johannesburg: University of Witwatersrand

Lappeman J, Ransome K & Louw Z (2019) Not one segment: Using global and local BoP characteristics to model country-specific consumer profiles. *European Business Review*, 31(3): 317–336

Lewis C & Piles S (1996) Woman, body, space: Rio carnival and the politics of performance. *Gender, Place, and Culture*, 3(1): 23–41

Ludden D (2019) *Night owls have more sex, morning larks have more children*. Accessed 20 September 2019, https://www.psychologytoday.com/za/blog/talking-apes/201909/night-owls-have-more-sex-morning-larks-have-more-children

Lugones M (1987) Playfulness, 'World'-Travelling, and Loving Perception. *Hyptia*, 2(2): 3–19

Lury C (1996) *Consumer culture*. New Jersey: Rutgers University Press

Mabandla N (2013) Lahla Ngubo: The continuities and discontinuities of a South African black middle class. Master's dissertation. Cape Town: University of Cape Town

Mabena G (2017) 'Loxion management': Social networks and precarious economies, a case study of Thembisa. Master's dissertation. Johannesburg: University of Witwatersrand

Magubane Z (2004) *Bringing the empire home: Race, class, and gender in Britain and colonial South Africa*. Chicago: University of Chicago Press

Maldini I & Manz L (2017) From 'Things of imitation' to 'devices of differentiation': Uncovering a paradoxical history of clothing (1950–2015). *Fashion Theory*, 22(1): 69–84

Malinga M & Ratele K (2016) 'It's cultivated, grown, packaged and sold with a price tag': Young black men's consumption of media messages of love, happiness, and constructions of masculinity. *Culture, Society & Masculinities*, 8(2): 100–117

McCracken G (1990) *Culture and consumption*. Indiana: Indiana University

Mchunu K (2016) *Izikhothane* youth phenomenon: The Janus face of contemporary culture in South Africa. *African Identities*, 1(11): 132–142

Melber H (ed.) (2017) *The rise of Africa's middle class: Myths, realities and critical engagements*. Johannesburg: Wits University Press

Memela B (2018) 'Swag': An ethnographic study of *izikhothane* fashion identity. Master's dissertation. Durban: Durban University of Technology

Merton RK (1938) Social structure and anomie. *American Sociological Review*, 3(5): 672–682

Mkhwanazi P (2011) Conspicuous consumption and black youth in emerging markets. Master's dissertation. Pretoria: University of Pretoria

Mnisi J (2015) Burning to consume? *Izikhothane* in Daveyton as aspirational consumers. *Communicatio: South African Journal of Communication Theory and Research*, 42(3): 340–353

Mnisi J (2019) Booty on fire: Looking at *izikhothane* with Thorstein Veblen. In D Posel & I Van Wyk (eds) *Conspicuous consumption in Africa*. Johannesburg: Wits University Press

Mnisi JG & Ngcongo M (2023) Looking back to look forward: Re-humanization through conspicuous consumption in four African masculine sartorial subcultures – from diamond field's dandies to *izikhothane*. *Africa Identities*, 21(2): 341–354

Moav O & Neeman Z (2010) Saving rates and poverty: The role of conspicuous consumption and human capital. *Journal of the European Economic Association*, 8(2–3): 413–420

Moav O & Neeman Z (2008) *Conspicuous Consumption, Human Capital, and Poverty*. Accessed 3 March 2012, https://ssrn.com/abstract=1140634 or http://dx.doi.org/10.2139/ssrn.1140634

Modisane B (1963) *Blame me on history*. New York: EP Dutton

Mohamed K (2011) Refashioning the local: Black masculinity, class and clothing. *Agenda*, 25(4): 104–111

Moller AC, Deci EL & Ryan RM (2010) Interpersonal control, dehumanization, and violence: A self-determination theory perspective. *Group Processes & Intergroup Relations*, 13(1) 41–53

Morrell R, Jewkes R & Lindegger G (2012) Hegemonic masculinity/masculinities in South Africa: Culture, power, and gender politics. *Men and Masculinities*, 15: 11–30

Mzobe S (2010) *Young blood.* Cape Town: Kwela Books

Nachbar JH (1998) The last word on Giffen goods? *Economic Theory*, 11(2): 403–412

Narunsky-Laden S (2008) Identity in post-apartheid South Africa: 'Learning to belong' through the (commercial) media. In A Hadland, E Louw, S Sesanti & H Wasserman (eds) *Power, politics and identity in South African media.* Cape Town: HSRC Press

Nedelcu F (2009) *La SAPE – Fashion above everything.* Oddity Central (blog). Accessed 18 June 2013, http://www.odditycentral.com/pics/la-sape-fashion-above-everything.html

Ngcobo NB (2016) *S'khothane*: Representation in, and influence on, contemporary visual arts practices. Master's dissertation. Pretoria: University of South Africa

Nicole B (2003) The base of the pyramid (BOP): Reperceiving business from the bottom up. *Global Business Network (GBN) Working Paper.* Accessed 3 March 2012, https://grist.org/wp-content/uploads/2006/03/gbn_bop_paper.pdf

Nkosi L (2011) *Izikhothane* burn swag. *Mahala.* Accessed 3 March 2012, http://www.mahala.co.za

Nuttall S (2004) Stylizing the self: The Y Generation in Rosebank. Johannesburg. *Public Culture*, 16(3): 430–452

Nyanga M (2015) The nature of brand loyalty at the base of the pyramid. Master's dissertation. Tshwane: Gordon Institute of Business Science

Oelofsen R (2009) De- and rehumanization in the wake of atrocities. *South African Journal of Philosophy*, 28(2):178–188

Pernegger L & Godegart S (2017) *Townships in the South African geographic landscape – Physical and social legacies and challenges.* Training for Township Renewal Initiative (TTRI). Accessed 24 July 2019, https://www.treasury.gov.za/divisions/bo/ndp/ttri/ttri%20oct%202007/day%201%20-%2029%20oct%202007/1a%20keynote%20address%20li%20pernegger%20paper.pdf

Perry R (2007) *'Race' and racism: The development of modern racism in America*. New York: Palgrave MacMillan

Pettinger L (2017) Green collar work: Conceptualizing and exploring an emerging field work. *Sociology Compass*, 11(1): 33–50

Posel D & Van Wyk I (eds) (2019) *Conspicuous consumption in Africa*. Johannesburg: Wits University Press

Posel D (2010) Races to consume: Revisiting South Africa's history of race, consumption and the struggle for freedom. *Ethnic and Racial Studies*, 33(2): 157–175

Prahalad CK & Hammond A (2002) Serving the world's poor, profitably. *Harvard Business Review*, 80(9): 48–57

Prahalad CK & Hart SL (2002) The fortune at the bottom of the pyramid. *Strategy+Business*, 26(1): 2–14

Prahalad CK (2005) *The fortune at the base of the pyramid: Eradicating poverty through profits*. New Jersey: Wharton School Publishing

Prahalad CK (2012) Bottom of the pyramid as a source of breakthrough innovations. *Journal of Product Innovation Management*, 29(1): 6–12

Pruitt S (2016) *Where did the word 'barbarian' come from?* Sarah Pruitt stories on History.com website. Accessed 26 March 2019, https://www.history.com/news/where-did-the-word-barbarian-come-from

Pyyhtinen O (2018) *The Simmel legacy: A science of relations*. United Kingdom: Palgrave

Ramphoma S (2014) Understanding poverty: Causes, effects and characteristics. *Interim: Interdisciplinary Journal*, 13(2): 59–72

Ratele K (2012) '*Ayashisa amateki*: Converse All Stars and the making of African masculinities. In R Moletsane, C Mitchell & A Smith (eds) *Was it something I wore? Dress, identity, materiality*. Cape Town: HSRC Press

Ratele K (2014) Gender equality in the abstract and practice. *Men and Masculinities*, 17(5): 510–514

Ratele K (2015) Working through resistance in engaging boys and men towards gender equality and progressive masculinities. *Culture, Health & Sexuality: An International Journal for Research, Innovation and Care*, 17(2): 144–158

Reddy T (2000) *Hegemony and resistance: Contesting identities in South Africa*. Farnham: Ashgate

Redhead S (1990) *The end of the century party: Youth and pop towards 2000*. Manchester: Manchester University Press

Richards JG & Langa M (2018) *Izikhothane*: Class and masculinities of black male youths in Katlehong Township, South Africa. *South African Review Sociology*, 49(2): 86–104

Richards JG (2015) *Izikhothane*: Masculinity and class in Katlehong, a South African township. Master's dissertation. Johannesburg: University of Witwatersrand

Saad G & Vongas JG (2009) The effect of conspicuous consumption on men's testosterone levels. *Organizational Behavior and Human Decision Processes*, 110: 80–92

SASSA (2023) *A statistical summary of social grants in South Africa*. Accessed 3 May 2024, https://www.sassa.gov.za/statistical-reports/Documents/FACT%20SHEET%20%20March%202023.pdf

Sassatelli R (2007) *Consumer culture: History, theory and politics*. London: Sage

Scheetz T (n.d.) *A modern investigation of status consumption*. Accessed 14 May 2014, https://artscimedia.case.edu/wp-content/uploads/sites/57/2014/01/14235806/scheetzreport.pdf

Seyyedi H & Akhlaghi E (2013) The study of onomatopoeia in the Muslims' Holy Writ: Qur'an. *Language in India*, 13(4): 16–24

Simmel G (1957) Fashion. *The American Journal of Sociology*, 62(6): 541–558 (Original work published in 1904. *International Quarterly*, 10(22): 130–150)

Simmel, G. (1904/1957). Fashion. *The American Journal of Sociology*, 62(6): 541 – 558. http://www.modetheorie.de/fileadmin/Texte/s/Simmel-Fashion_1904.pdf

Simpson J & Lappeman J (eds) (2017) *Marketing in South Africa* (4th ed.). Pretoria: Van Schaik

Sonti VM (2020) UPSpace Institutional Repository, Department of Library Services, University of Pretoria. Accessed 16 February 2023, https://repository.up.ac.za/handle/2263/87267

South African History Online (2019) *Thembisa Township, Midrand*. Accessed 14 September 2019, https://www.sahistory.org.za/place/Thembisa-township-midrand

Southall R (2016) *The new black middle class in South Africa*. Johannesburg: Jacana Media

Spacey J (2017) *6 types of aspirational brands*. Accessed 9 October 2019, https://simplicable.com/new/aspirational-brand

Srivastava A, Mukherjee S & Jebarajakirthy C (2021) Triggers of aspirational consumption at the base of the Pyramid: A qualitative inquiry from Indian context. *Journal of Strategic Marketing*, 31(1): 154–184

Subhan F & Khattak A (2017) *What constitutes the bottom of the pyramid (BOP) market?* Accessed 4 April 2019, https://www.researchgate.net/publication/315744411_What_Constitutes_the_Bottom_of_the_Pyramid_BOP_Market

Sullivan A (2001) Cultural capital and educational attainment. *Sociology*, 35(4): 893–912

Tarde, G (1903) *Laws of imitation*, 2nd ed. New York: Henry Holt

Taylor G & Spencer S (2004) *Social identities: A multidisciplinary approach*. New York: Routledge

Trapido A (2008) *Hunger for freedom: The story of food in the life of Nelson Mandela*. Johannesburg: Jacana Media

Tullock C (2010). Style-fashion-dress: From black to post-black. *Fashion Theory*, 14(3): 273–304

Turner J, Beeghley L, Noad J & Powers CH (2002) The emergence of sociological theory. *Teaching Sociology*, 28(4): 406–416

TVSA (2012) *Jaw Dropped By Izikhothane - Reloaded*. Accessed 2025, https://www.tvsa.co.za/user/blogs/viewblogpost.aspx?blogpostid=29743#google_vignette

Vagvolyi R, Coldea A, Dresler T, Schrader J & Huerk H (2016) A review about functional illiteracy: Definition, cognitive, linguistic, and numerical aspects. *Frontiers in Psychology*, 7(1617): 1–13

Vanthemsche G (2006) The historiography of Belgian colonialism in the Congo. In C Levai (ed.) *Europe and the world in European historiography* (pp. 89-119). Edizioni Plus, Pisa University: Pisa. Accessed 10 November 2013, http://www.cliohres.net/books/6/Vanthemsche.pdf

Veblen T (1899/2003) *The theory of the leisure class*. Lewiston: Edwin Mellen Press (Original work published in 1899. New York: Macmillan)

Viljoen S (2008) Masculine ideals in post-apartheid South Africa: The rise of men's glossies. In A Hadland, E Louw, S Sesanti & H Wasserman (eds) *Power, politics, and identity in post-apartheid South African media*. Cape Town: HSRC Press

Viswanathan M, Rosa JA & Harris J (2005) Decision-making and coping by functionally illiterate consumers and some implications for marketing management. *Journal of Marketing*, 69(1): 15–31

Warnke G (2007) *After identity: Rethinking race, sex, and gender*. Cambridge: Cambridge University Press

Wehmeier S, McIntosh C, Turnbull J & Ashby M (eds) (2007) *Oxford advanced learner's dictionary: International student's edition*. New York: Oxford University Press

West C (2001) *Race matters*. Boston: Beacon Press

Willemse M, Smith MR & Padmanabhanunni A (2018) Exploring an historically disadvantaged South African tertiary institution's culture and response to providing reasonable accommodation to students diagnosed with ADHD. *South African Journal of Higher Education*, 32(6): 300–317

Wilson M (2003) Rhetoric of enrolment and acts of resistance: Information technology as text. In E Wynn, E Whitley, MD Myers & J De Gross (eds) *Global and organizational discourse about information technology*. Dordrecht: Kluwer Academic Publishers

Winant H (2000) Race and race theory. *Annual Review of Sociology*, 26: 169–185

Winkler R (2017) The long walk from 'civilised' and 'barbaric' to a new world view. *The Conversation*, 27 July. Accessed 26 March 2019, https://theconversation.com/the-long-walk-from-civilised-and-barbaric-to-a-new-world-view-81110

World Economic Forum (2009) *The global competitiveness report: 2009–2010*. Accessed 20 April 2019, http://www3.weforum.org/docs/WEF_GlobalCompetitivenessReport_2009-10.pdf

Zahavi A (1975) Mate selection: A selection for a handicap. *Journal of Theoretical Biology*, 53: 205–214

About the Author

Dr Sifiso JG Mnisi is the Head of the School of Communication at the University of Johannesburg, with a PhD in Communication Studies. His research interests span gender studies, media and communication, economic sociology, and the township lives of black male youths. With a deep commitment to interdisciplinary scholarship, Sifiso explores the intersections of identity, media representation, and socioeconomic structures in shaping contemporary social experiences. His work critically examines how communication and media influence societal narratives, particularly in marginalized communities. As an academic leader, he is dedicated to fostering innovative research and advancing knowledge in the dynamic field of communication studies.

Index

Notes are indexed.

A
Acts
    Group Areas Act of 1950 3, 42
    Natives Land Act 27 of 1913 128
    Representation of Natives Act of 1936 85, 127
    Union of South Africa 1936, section 41 127, 128
Acquired Immune Deficiency Syndrome (AIDS) 100
African National Congress 128
age 1, 6, 59, 60, 100, 101, 117, 130, 131, 132, 134, 138, 143
alcohol 1, 12, 14, 37, 56, 60, 63, 66, 67, 71, 72, 94, 113, 123, 126, 130, 131, 143
    see also brand conscious
amangamla 105
amapantsulas see *pantsula*
anti-consumerism *see* consumption
apartheid 54, 57, 84, 107, 113, 116
    post- 1, 2, 3, 4, 5, 8, 10, 13, 15, 17, 18, 32, 45, 47, 57, 78, 103, 112, 117, 127, 143, 144
    pre- 52
    regime/government 4, 39, 42, 49, 52, 61, 104, 112, 126, 128
    see also colonial(ism)
aspiration(al) 2, 4, 8, 9, 12, 14, 19, 21, 39, 42, 44, 45, 48, 58, 71, 72, 78, 79, 80, 89, 91, 99, 107, 108, 110, 111, 112, 118, 129, 142, 144
    consumption 43, 61, 75, 78–84, 112, 140, 142, 144
    masculinities 103, 112–115, 119, 124, 142
    see also masculine

B
base of the pyramid *see* bottom of the pyramid
behaviour 1, 3, 8, 16, 22, 25, 44, 50, 63, 72, 75, 80, 91, 92, 96, 116, 124
    see also *izikhothane*
    consumption 25, 26, 43, 4, 75, 76 79
    destructive/deviant 9, 18, 19 22, 45
    human 91, 97, 99
Birch Acres 4, 5, 6, 83, 89

black diamonds 10
black people 3, 12, 42, 48, 49, 54, 61, 62, 77, 84, 85, 88, 103, 116, 126, 128, 129, 132
black tax 46n5
booty 63, 69, 74, 142
BoP *see* bottom of the pyramid (BoP)
bottom of the pyramid (BoP) 45, 78, 79, 82, 84, 111, 112, 115, 118
    consumer consumption 33–36
    characteristics 36–40
    South African specific 40–42
    population segment 35, 36, 39, 42, 43, 44, 47, 87, 88
brand consciousness 32, 38, 39, 40, 42, 76, 80, 115, 139
    alcohol 1, 63, 123
    clothing 48, 62, 73, 74, 77, 83, 116, 117, 134, 136, 138, 142
    see also clothes
    food 57, 63, 64, 67, 69. 83
burn events 1, 15, 63, 65, 66, 67, 70, 72, 75, 82, 140
    see also clothes

C
carnivalesque 15
cash backs 5
CCCS *see* University of Birmingham's Centre for Contemporary Cultural studies (CCCS)
cigarettes *see* smoking
citizenship 13, 119, 126
    class 19, 20, 21, 27, 28, 49, 54, 58, 62, 63, 68, 73, 76, 85, 104, 112, 116, 117, 118
    aspirational 4, 78, 117
classless 29
    distinction 27, 28, 29, 30, 104
    elite 26, 27, 28, 30, 32, 78
    leisure 7, 27, 28, 54, 61, 63, 66, 67, 72, 73, 74, 75–78, 81, 124, 141
    lower 28, 29, 63, 67, 68, 74, 117, 123, 141, 142
    middle 4, 5, 37, 40, 42, 46n5, 48, 49, 77, 78, 105, 116, 117, 135
    problems 19, 20, 135
    social 5, 16, 19, 28, 30, 48, 56, 62, 67, 105, 106, 112, 116
    upper 27, 29, 30, 41, 78, 117, 118
    working 2, 14, 19, 28, 37, 54, 56, 63, 64, 68, 73, 103
clothes 7, 22, 30, 37, 39, 40, 53, 54, 56, 60, 63, 65, 66, 68, 70, 71, 72, 73, 74, 83, 84, 86, 97, 98, 106, 109, 114, 118, 119, 128, 130, 143

INDEX

destruction/burning of 10, 14, 21, 22, 63, 66, 72, 140, 141
expensive 1, 12, 14, 17, 30, 32, 39, 59, 64, 67, 69, 73, 74, 98, 104, 113, 114, 123, 140, 141
  see also brand consciousness
collective action 138
  distraction from 139
colonial(ism) 49, 52, 54, 84, 85, 104, 107, 126, 128
  see also apartheid
conspicuous consumption 6, 7, 26, 27, 28, 31, 45, 47–48, 66–69, 75–78, 81, 83, 92–95, 97, 102, 123, 124, 129
  see also consumption
  destructive 1, 2, 7, 8, 9, 63, 122
  see also Veblen
  social psychology 92–95
  township, 9–13
consumerism *see* consumption
consumption (behaviour)
  see also conspicuous consumption
  as communication message 69, 136
  aspirational 43, 61, 75, 78, 79, 80, 81, 82, 84, 89, 112, 140, 142, 144
complex nature 18, 24
contextual 13–14
  demand and supply 2, 24, 25, 26, 76, 91
  elite/wealthy 32 33
  media representation 115–119
  patterns 24, 32, 36, 43, 48, 67, 69, 75, 79, 80, 82, 88, 104, 112, 115, 126, 127, 136
  shortfalls 138–139, 146
  social change 30, 48, 126–129
  status wealth 26, 80, 81, 124
criminal activities 6, 64
cultural capital 17, 113, 134–135
culture 14, 17, 53, 54
  youth 15, 20, 21, 69, 74, 110, 142

D

dance(ing) 6, 13, 20, 22, 65, 66, 70, 71, 88, 97, 98, 111, 114, 132, 143
dandy(ism) 52, 53, 54, 58, 73, 104, 141
dating 65, 96, 106, 123, 131
  see also relationships
Daveyton 47, 56, 58, 79, 103, 115
  see also townships

dehumanisation 39, 47, 49, 50, 51, 52, 53, 54, 56, 57, 61, 62, 85, 112, 123, 128
  see also rehumanisation
  through race 50–52
delinquency 19
destructive(tion) 2, 7, 9, 10, 11, 14, 15, 18, 21, 22, 63, 65, 68, 74, 114, 139, 140, 141
  see also wasteful(ness)
deviant behaviour 18, 19, 22, 45
diamond fields dandies *see* dandy(ism)
dignity 11, 39, 40, 42, 50, 54, 58, 59, 61, 84, 85, 128, 129, 136
  see also honour, respect
dissing 1, 9, 12, 13, 59, 114
dress *see* fashion

E
economy(cally) 2, 10, 15, 26, 34, 36, 40, 41, 62, 71, 75, 78, 84, 116
  education 8, 13, 37, 38, 42, 43, 56, 57, 78, 85, 87, 88, 105, 115, 121, 127,
    129, 130, 131, 132, 133, 134, 135, 142
ekasi 60, 87, 107, 108
emulation model *see* Simmel, Veblen
entrepreneurship 129
  economic implications 136–138
events 1, 8, 15, 16, 40, 65, 72, 98, 103, 114, 119, 123, 133
  see also *izikhothane*

F
fame *see* honour
fashion style 6, 18, 20, 22, 32, 39, 47, 53, 54, 55, 61, 86, 108, 117, 128, 136
  diffusion lines 76, 77
females *see* women
food 1, 4, 11, 25, 43, 57, 62, 67, 69, 84, 106, 123
  see also brand consciousness
fragmentation of efforts 128, 139
freedom 48, 49, 62, 84, 101, 109, 126, 129, 130

G
gender 12, 49, 50, 58, 62, 79, 91, 92, 93, 94, 113, 123, 131
Giffen goods 24, 25
girls/girlfriends *see* women
goals 12, 19, 38, 44, 45, 47, 72, 73, 110, 144

H
handicap principle 93, 94, 96, 97, 99, 102

INDEX

hierarchy of needs pyramid (Abraham Maslow) 84
   inverted pyramid 85
honour 26, 27, 31, 39, 44, 63, 66, 67, 69, 73, 74, 75, 96, 115, 122, 141, 142
   see also dignity, respect
Human Immunodeficiency Virus (HIV) 100
hustle(rs) 13, 37, 64, 70, 74, 86, 122, 123, 130, 131, 134, 136, 137, 142

I

identities 2, 8, 16, 20, 26, 49, 50, 57, 69, 92, 104, 107, 109, 116, 136, 142
   consumption 47, 57, 68, 74, 89
   desired 9, 11, 40, 53, 58, 79, 87, 109, 112, 113, 123
   formation 9, 10, 17
   gender 79, 92, 94, 102
   masculine 45, 58, 112, 114, 115, 116, 117, 122, 124, 132, 133, 143, 144
   social 7, 47, 117, 118
imitation see Simmel
impoverishment 2, 11, 15, 16, 47, 73, 83, 94, 117, 124, 135
industrial(isation) 26, 27, 31, 66
Industrial Revolution 54, 76, 77
inequalities 4, 5, 9, 13, 21, 27, 39, 41, 57, 62, 66, 89, 116, 129, 139
ingamla 86, 103, 104, 105, 108
   see also umlungu
inkunzi 96
izikhothane
   behaviour 1, 16, 18, 26, 45, 75, 79, 89, 94, 95, 136
   contextual consumption 13–14
   desire through resistance 14–16, 21
   family background 2, 41, 64, 73, 94, 122, 135
   gatherings 1, 65, 66
   see also events
incentives 139
   lifestyle funding 2, 8, 13, 33, 37, 64, 65, 70, 93, 94, 136, 142
   neo-tribe 17, 18, 20, 21
   performances 64–66, 74
   see also masculinities, The Good Fellas, *ukukhothana*, Veblen, women
   subculture 18–23, 113, 114
   Thembisa 69–72

J

Janus face 13, 14
Jewishing 83, 89n2

L
La Sape 52, 53, 55, 56, 58
lifestyles 13, 14, 56, 57, 60, 64, 68, 74, 81, 82, 114, 115, 136, 137, 141, 142
liquor *see* alcohol
literacy/illiteracy 38
lived experiences 2, 112, 129
luxury goods 1, 17, 26, 27, 30, 48, 55, 63, 67, 76, 139

M
males 1, 2, 6, 9, 13, 19, 47, 54, 55, 58, 85, 93, 112, 114, 118, 123, 127
   see also men
Mandela, Nelson 11, 105, 109, 128
manhood 58, 61, 113, 115, 122, 124, 130, 131, 132, 143, 144
marginalisation 9, 47, 52, 57, 58, 75, 89, 116, 130, 136
masculine identity *see* identities
masculine(ities) 24, 45, 47, 54, 71, 73, 91, 101, 102, 124, 130, 140, 143
   see also aspiration
   citizen 119–124
   consumption 58–62
   hegemonic 45, 112, 114, 116, 117, 124, 131, 143, 144
   hyper- 114, 131
media representation 115–119
matric *see* education
media 2, 7, 8, 11, 14, 17, 18, 39, 40, 68, 69, 75, 87, 115–119, 143
men 12, 26, 54, 55, 58, 60, 66, 71, 72, 83, 94, 95, 100, 101, 106, 114, 115, 123
   see also males
   black 62, 74, 116, 117, 141
   South African 53, 54, 61
   young 2, 10, 11, 62, 63, 64, 65, 67, 68, 69, 73, 74, 117, 136, 141
mineworkers 54, 104
Miss Masakhane Beauty Pageant 65, 99, 101, 109, 119, 122
music 1, 6, 12, 20, 22, 65, 66, 126

N
National Party 3, 84, 128
natives 85, 127, 128
   non- 85, 127
nightlife 10, 12, 71, 72, 95, 100, 101, 123, 130, 143

O
oswenka 52, 53, 54, 55, 58, 74, 141

INDEX

P
pantsula 6
parents 2, 8, 37, 41, 56, 64, 68, 87, 88, 101, 123, 132, 134, 135, 136, 137, 142
parks 16, 65
parties 11, 12, 13, 66, 73, 101, 118, 123, 130, 141
partners *see* women
paternalism 57
patriarchal 12, 45, 58, 95, 114, 115, 143, 144
performances 2, 8, 14, 16, 24, 27, 38, 40, 45, 53, 63, 64, 65, 68, 71, 72, 74, 86, 112, 141, 142
    gender 91, 92
    masculine 45, 101, 102, 117, 122, 130, 144
performative(ity) 31, 91–92, 102, 117, 129, 131
aesthetic 15, 18, 21
pexas 7
pexing 7, 8
post-apartheid *see* apartheid
post-subcultural theory 17, 18, 19, 149
    shortfalls 20–21
postmodern(ism) 7, 17, 18, 20
    potlatches 66, 67
poverty 2, 5, 7, 8, 9, 11, 13, 14, 15, 16, 21, 22, 33, 34, 35, 36, 38, 39, 42, 43, 45, 57, 62, 64, 69, 73, 74, 80, 89, 108, 116, 123, 129, 141, 142
PPP *see* purchasing power parity (PPP)
pre-apartheid *see* apartheid
pregnancy 99, 100, 101, 119
products 7, 8, 14, 25, 26, 76, 77, 80, 81, 87, 115
    see also alcohol, clothes, food
purchasing power parity (PPP) 35, 36, 41

R
Rabbi Letageng Youth Foundation (RLYF) 109, 120, 121
race(ial) 47, 49, 50–52, 54, 57, 62, 85, 103, 104, 109, 111–112, 116, 117, 126, 128, 127
rehumanisation 47, 49, 50, 52, 61, 85, 112, 123, 129
    see also dehumanisation
    sartorial expression 53–58
    see also sartorial
    steps to 50
relationships (human) 94, 95, 96, 97, 99, 100, 101, 118, 123, 124
    see also dating
resistance 14–16, 18, 19, 21, 45, 140, 141

respect 1, 19, 13, 27, 39, 55, 58, 59, 61, 64, 66, 69, 71, 72, 74, 75, 84, 85, 96, 100, 117, 122, 123, 124, 130, 131, 142
   see also dignity, honour
RLYF see Rabbi Letageng Youth Foundation (RLYF)
role models 10, 13, 32, 86, 108, 133, 134
rush hours 100, 101, 123, 143

S
s'khothane 16, 17, 59, 60, 64, 69, 71, 72, 86, 88, 97, 100, 111, 114, 131, 132, 133
sartorial 47, 52, 54, 56, 57, 58, 61, 74, 118, 141
   see also rehumanisation
self-esteem see dignity
signalling 27, 28, 30, 39, 53, 61, 62, 66, 70, 75–78, 81, 93, 94, 95–99, 105, 116, 126
Simmel, George
   emulation model 28–30, 33, 45, 77, 111
   imitation 28, 29, 30, 31, 68
   trickle-down theory 30, 31, 48
social change 30, 48, 126, 127–129, 131, 138
social mobility see upward mobility
social status 7, 9, 10, 26, 28, 45, 55, 67, 74, 75, 76, 78, 80, 81, 82, 83, 122, 123, 124, 138, 141, 142, 143
socioeconomic issues 2, 26, 34, 49, 61, 65, 73, 89, 94, 95, 97, 109, 112, 121, 124, 129, 136, 138, 139
soft life 87
Soshanguve 7, 16
   see also townships
subculture 21, 22, 133
see also izikhuthane, ukukhothana
success 9, 10, 44, 49, 65, 71, 78, 79, 86, 88, 103
   colour of 111–112
symbols of 86, 104–109
   upward mobility 109–111

T
The Good Fellas 21, 83, 122–123, 129, 130, 141, 142
   'amacan't get' 83, 84
   background 5, 6, 21, 73
   behaviour 72, 73, 96, 99, 100, 119
   earn a living 70, 134, 137
   education 87, 88, 131–133
   expensive purchases 69, 70, 71, 74

Phomolong 4, 5, 122, 137
    see also, izikhothane, ukukhothana
    smoking 60, 71, 72, 138
    Vusimuzi 4, 5, 89
Thembisa 3-6, 16, 37, 41, 65, 69, 83, 104, 110, 119, 140
    see also townships
townships 4, 6, 7, 8, 9, 37, 42, 68, 78, 86, 89, 107-109
    see also Daveyton, Soshanguve, Thembisa
tripartite 47, 53
twenty-first century 24, 26

U
ukukhothana 45, 67, 71, 72, 74, 75, 140, 141, 144
    see also izikhothane, The Good Fellas
    academic perspectives 7-23
    aspirational consumption see aspiration(al)
    discursive resistance 21, 45, 140
    expressing desire through resistance 14-16
    in context 63-64
    modern spaces 16-18
    performative elements see performances, performativity
    see burn events, masculinities, media
    subculture 3, 9, 13, 14, 15, 16, 17, 18-23, 24, 45, 47, 56, 114, 136, 138, 139
umkhothana 56, 57
umlungu 103, 104
    see also *ingamla*
    University of Birmingham's Centre for Contemporary Cultural studies
        (CCCS) 19,140
upward mobility 9, 14, 31, 62, 104, 107, 114, 116, 127, 128
    see also success

V
Veblen, Thorstein 25, 26, 30, 63
    effect, 26, 27
    conspicuous leisure see conspicuous consumption
    emulation model 31, 32, 33, 45, 67, 68, 77, 111
    goods 24, 25, 26
    leisure class see class
    trickle-down theory 30, 31, 48
Via Daveytons 47, 56, 58, 59
violence 5, 11, 12, 49, 50, 62, 116, 117

W

wasteful(ness) 2, 3, 16, 30, 38, 48, 63, 67, 68, 71, 72, 73, 74, 75, 81, 87, 89, 129, 141
　see also destructive
white 51, 52, 54, 69, 85, 104, 112, 130, 135
　domination 51, 52, 61, 104, 129
　non-39
　people 39, 42, 86, 103, 104, 105, 107, 108
　suburbs 3, 41, 86, 104, 107, 108, 128
whiteness 51, 104, 105, 107, 109, 128
women 1, 8, 10, 12, 58, 59, 60, 64, 66, 69, 72, 92, 93, 94, 95, 96, 97, 98, 99, 100, 101, 105, 106, 113, 114, 119, 123, 124, 130, 131, 142, 143